HEARTS OF GOLD

ORIGINALLY TITLED

HE DONE HER WRONG

HEARTS OF GOLD

The GREAT AMERICAN NOVEL

AND NOT A WORD IN IT—NO MUSIC, TOO

by

MILT GROSS

ABBEVILLE PRESS • PUBLISHERS • NEW YORK

Printed and bound in the United States of America.

First Abbeville Press edition, 1983, an unabridged,
unaltered republication of the work originally
published in 1930 by Doubleday, Doran & Company, Inc.,
under the title *He Done Her Wrong*.

Library of Congress Cataloging in Publication Data

Gross, Milt, 1895-1953.
Hearts of gold.

1. Stories without words. I. Title.
PN6727.G76H4 1983 741.5'973 82-22718
ISBN 0-89659-367-3

HEARTS OF GOLD

FOREWORD: THEY LAUGHED WHEN I SAT DOWN TO DRAW A NOVEL, BUT THEY DIDN'T LAUGH WHEN I FIN —— OOPS! THAT DIDN'T SOUND SO GOOD. WELL ANYWAY, ONCE UPON A TIME ——

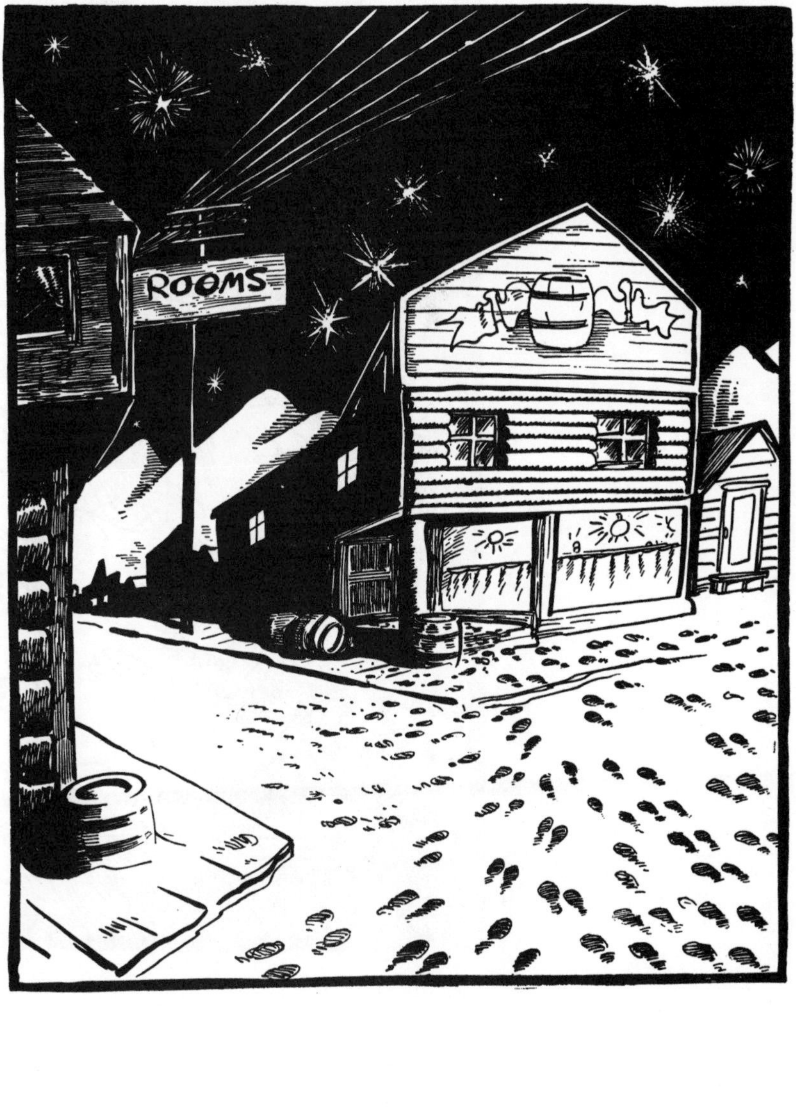
ROOMS

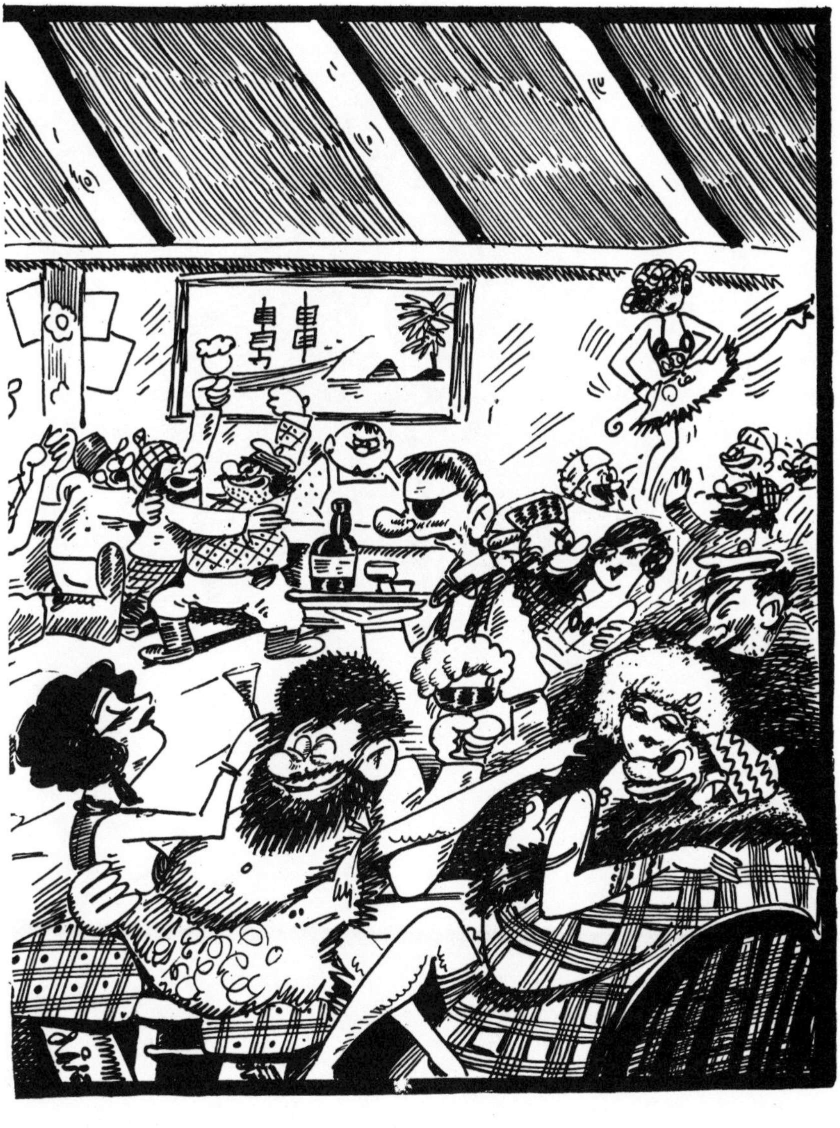

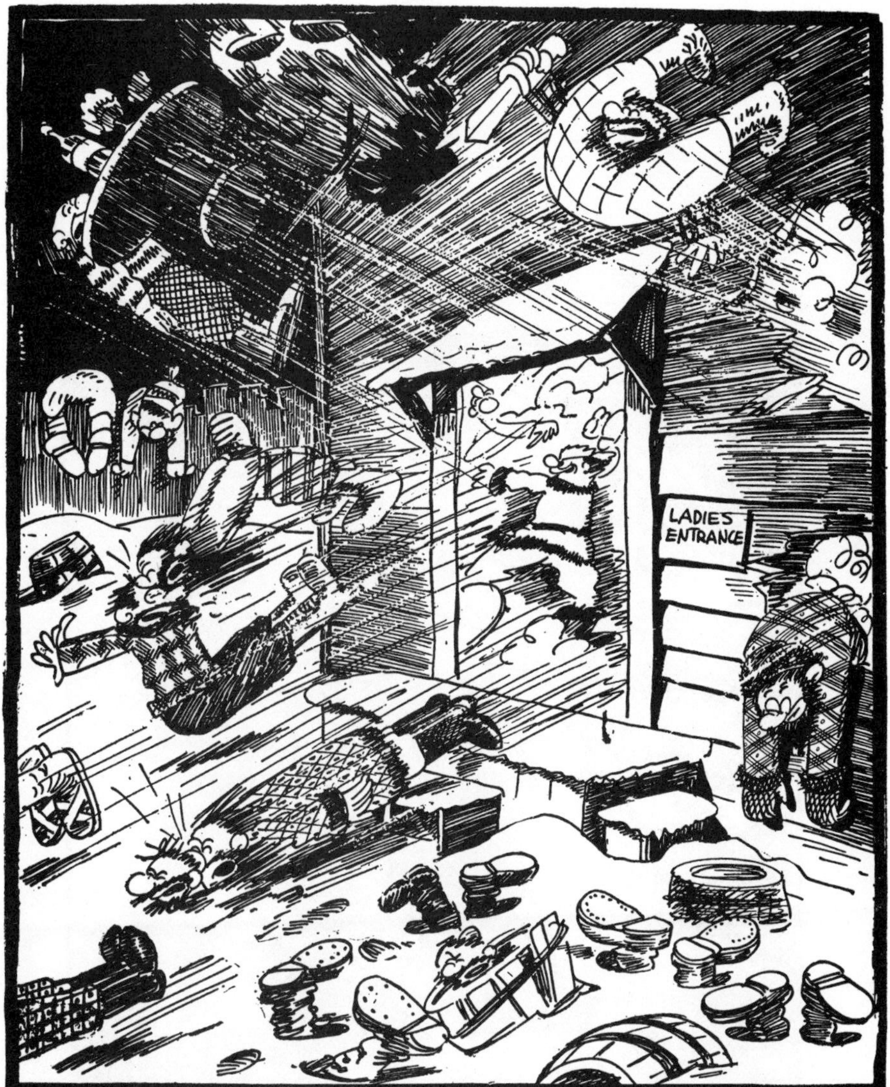
LADIES
ENTRANCE

15

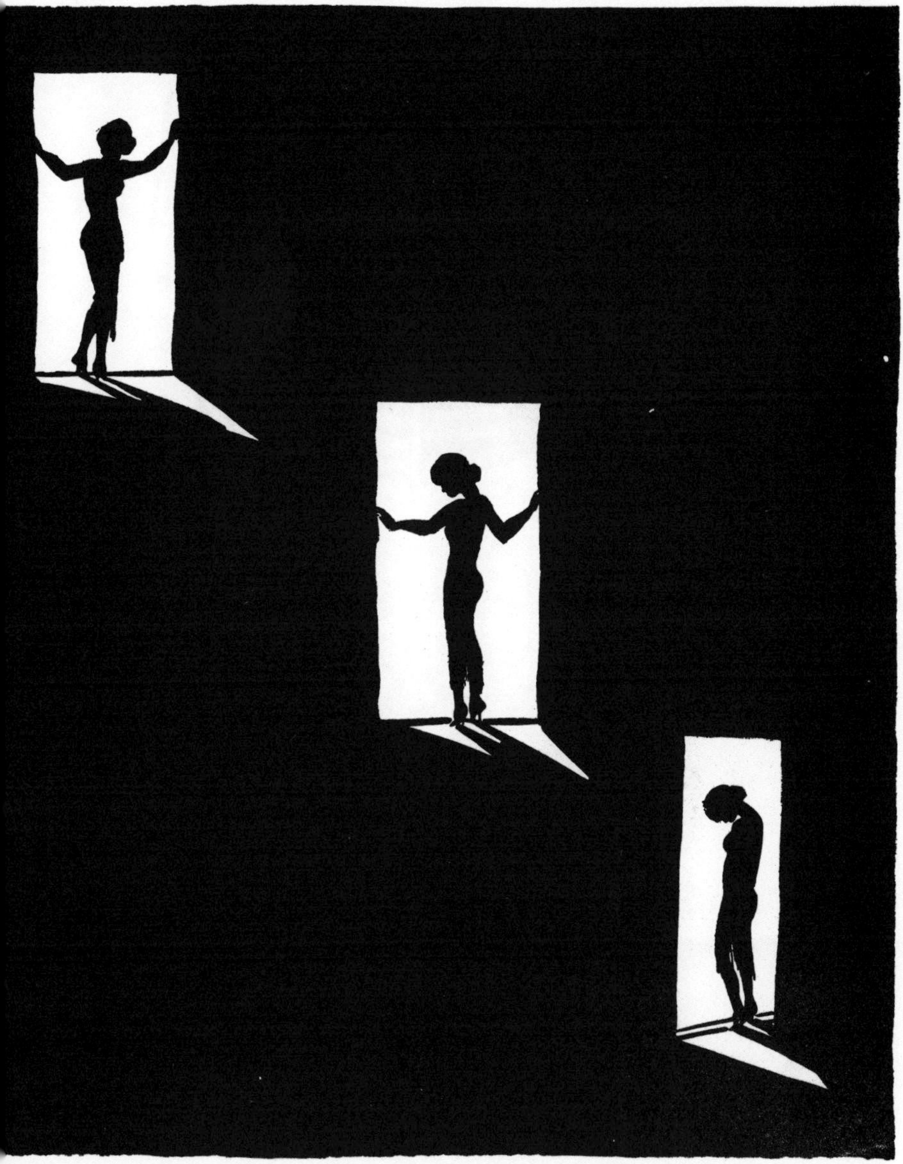

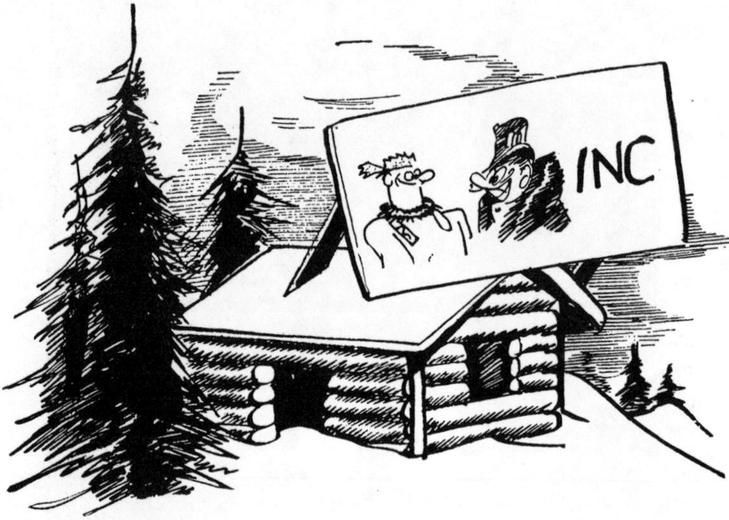
INC

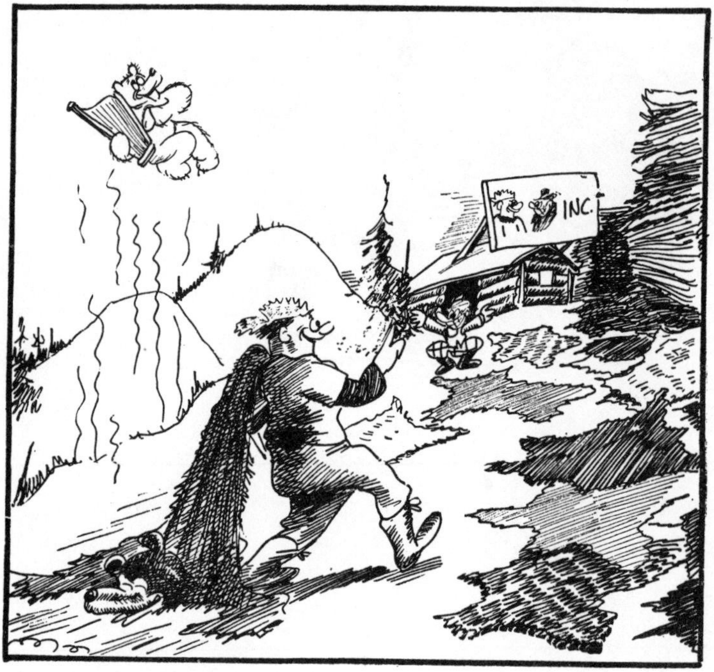
INC.

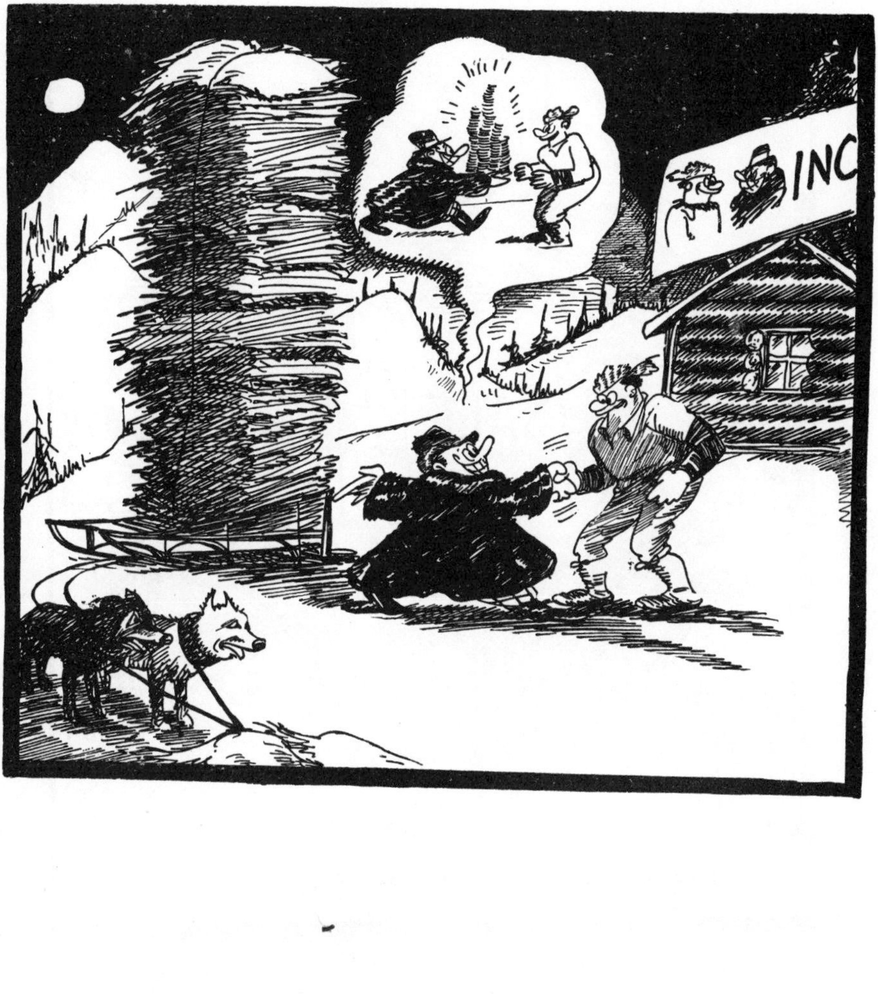
INC

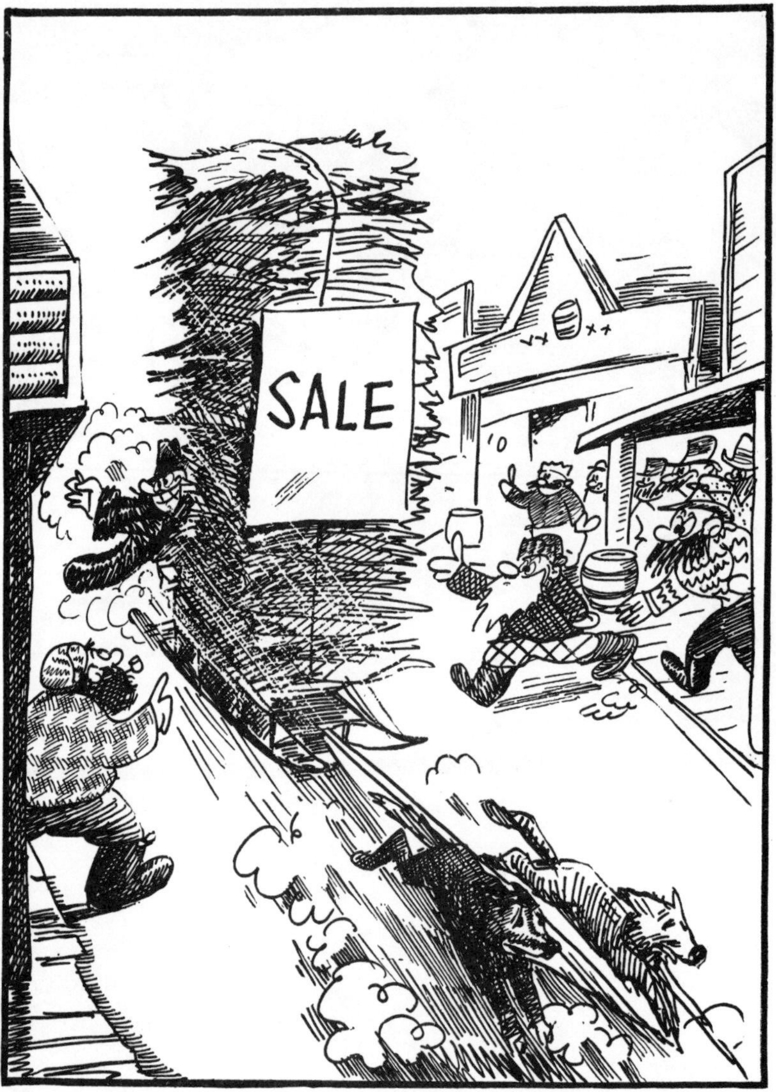
SALE

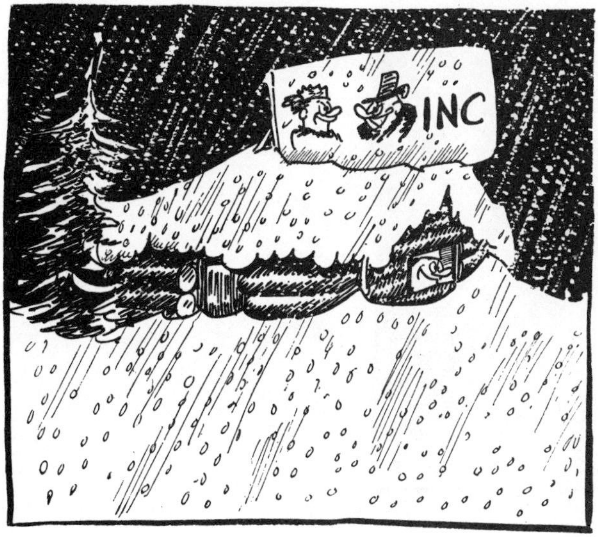
INC

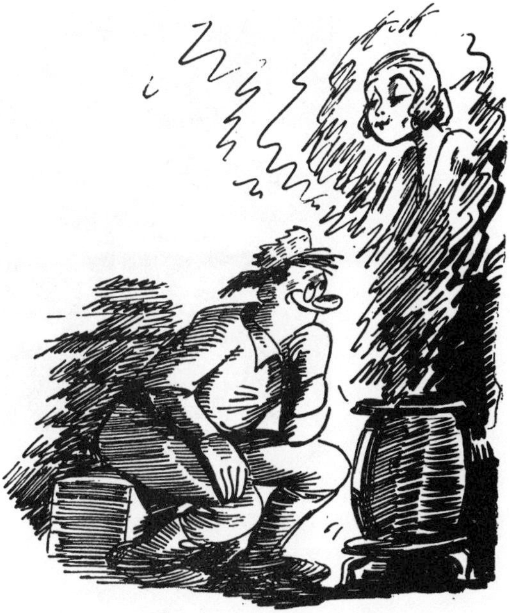

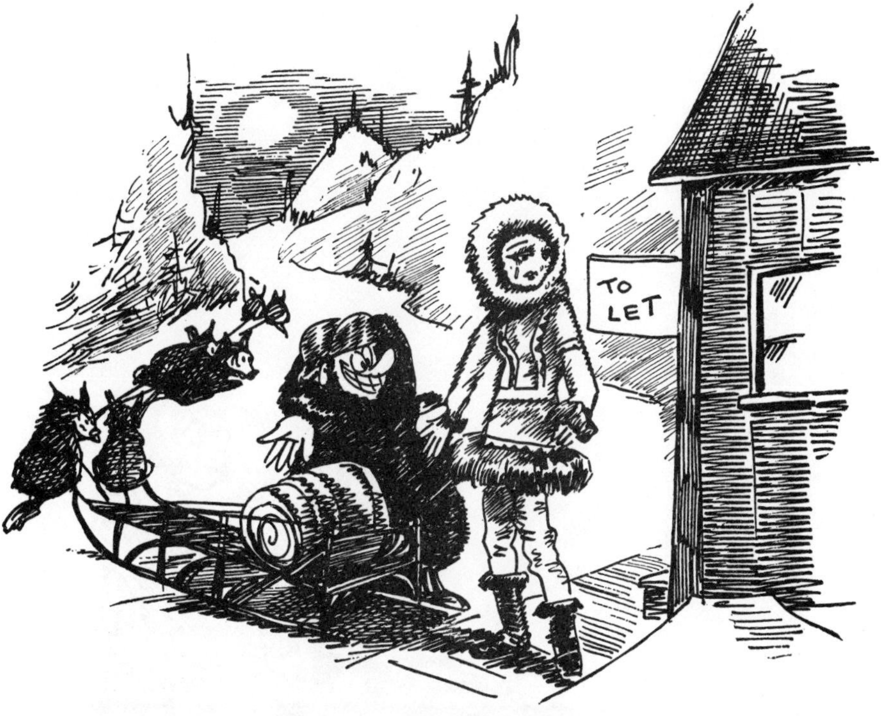
TO
LET

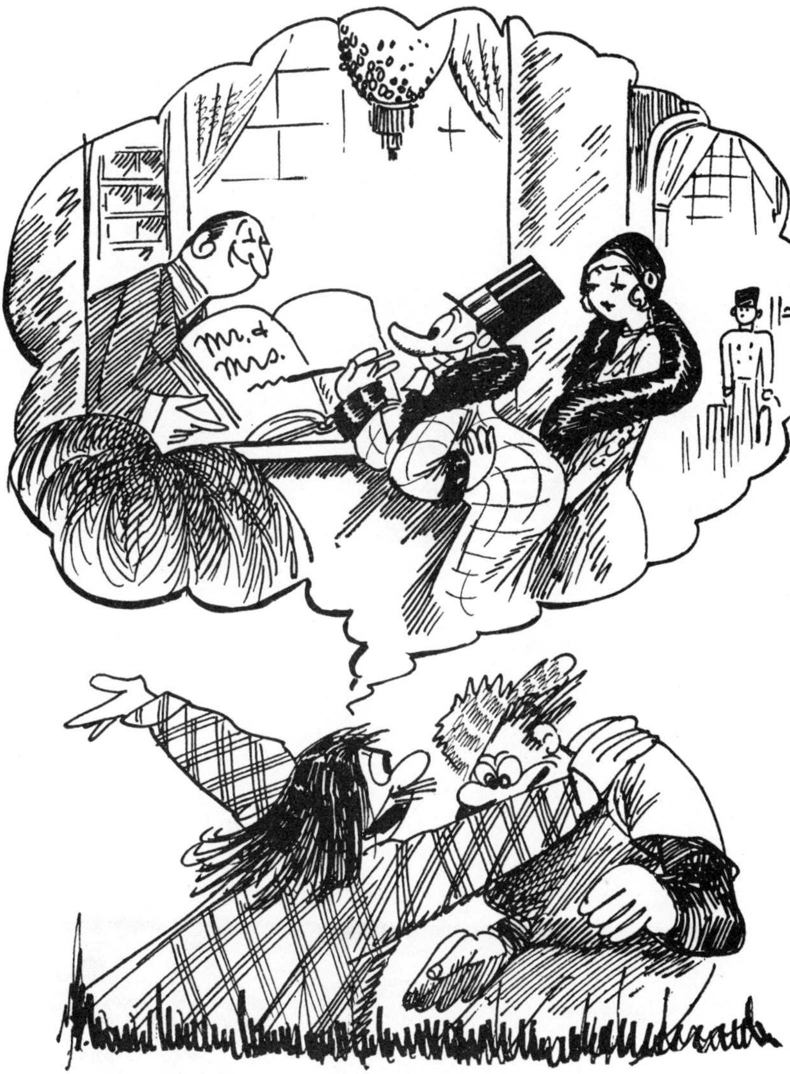
Mr. &
Mrs.

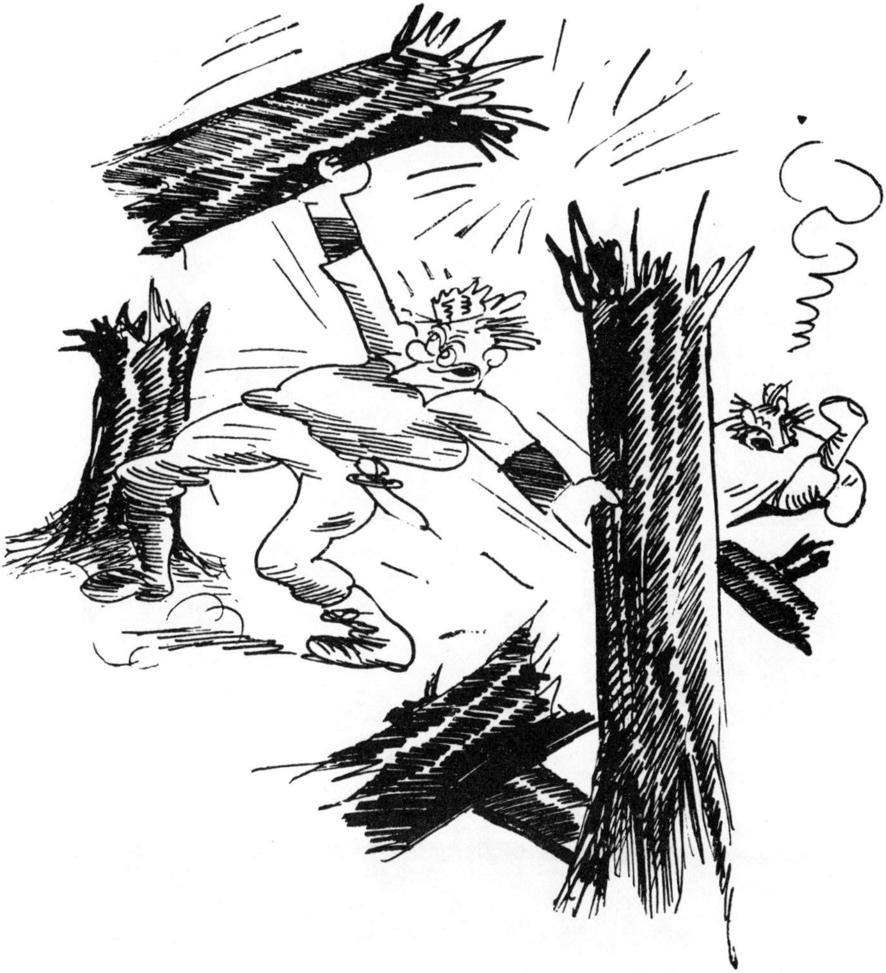

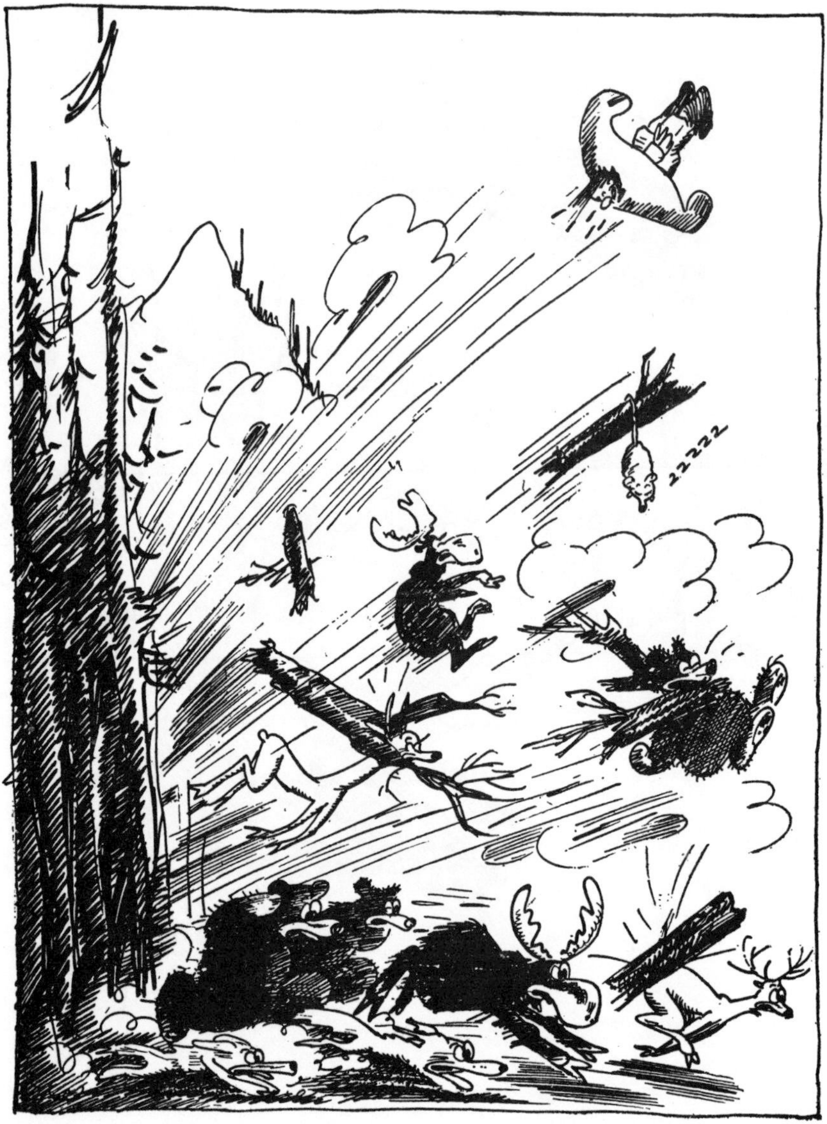
zzzzz

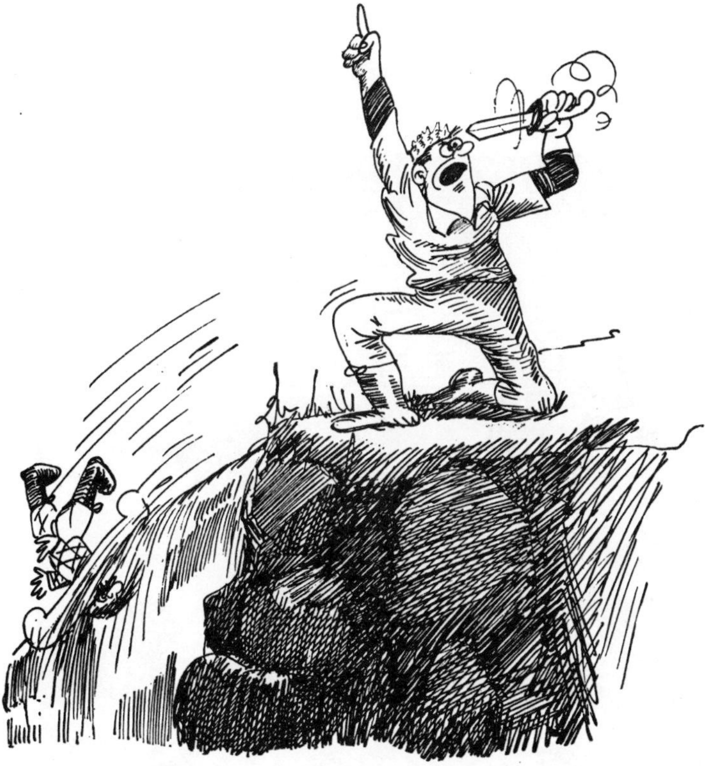

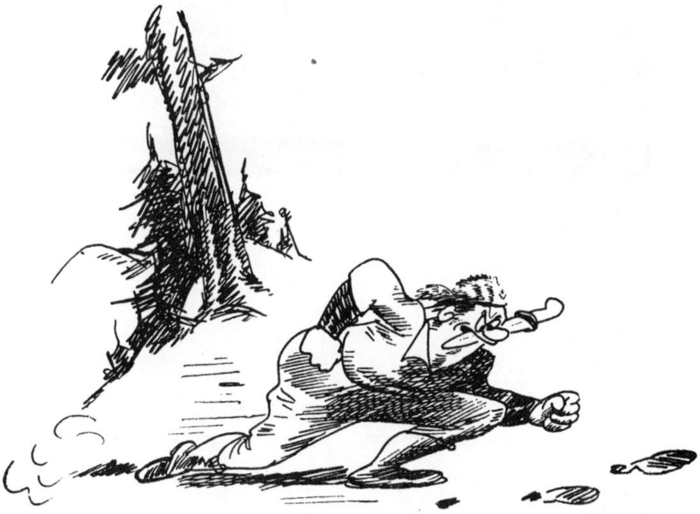

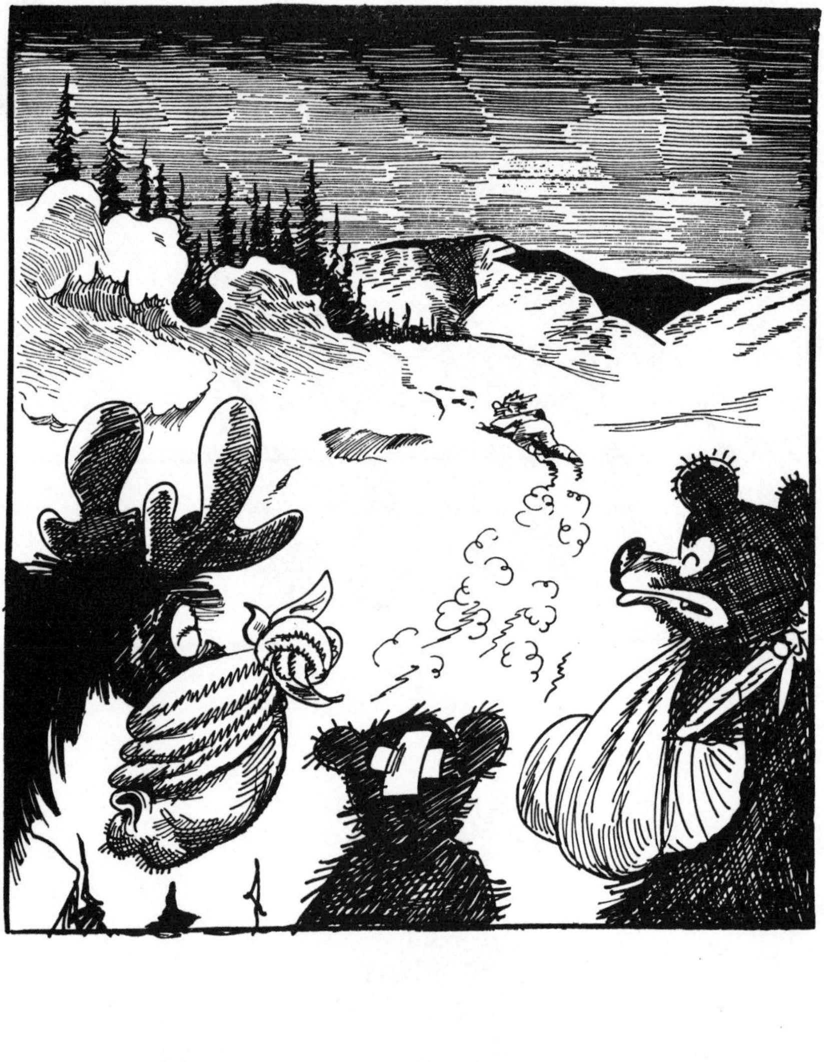

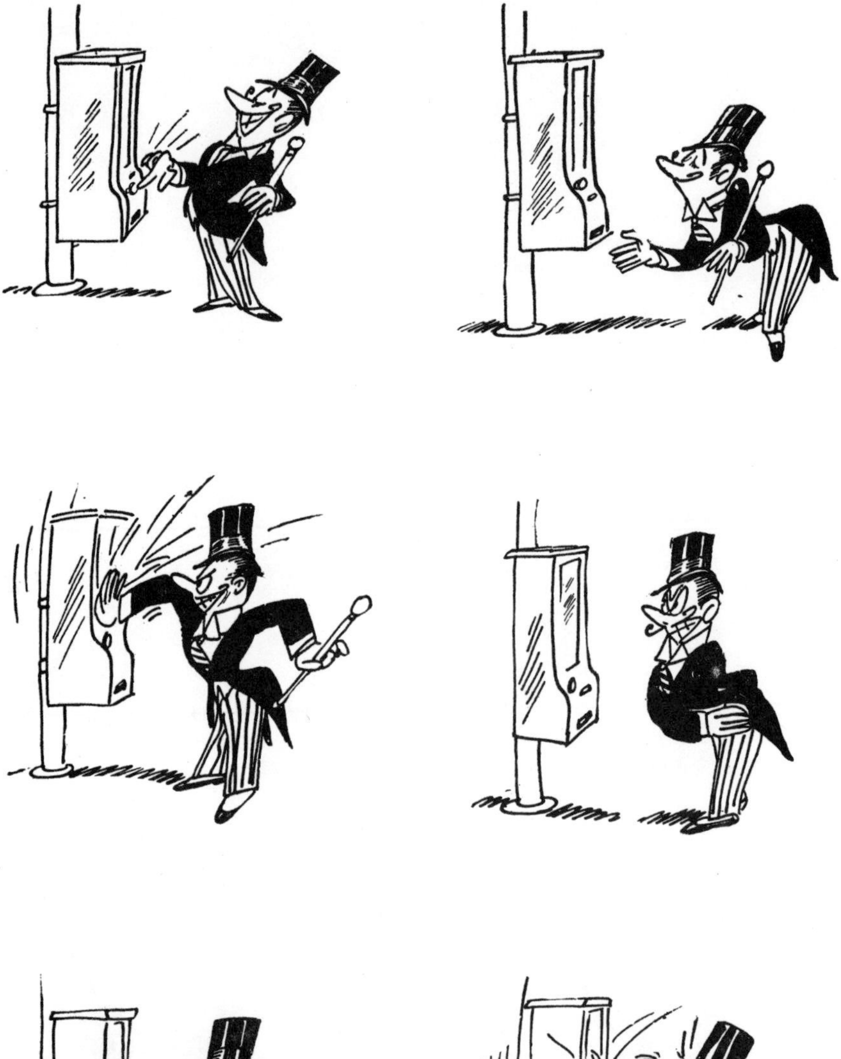

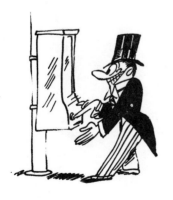

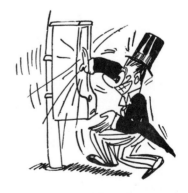

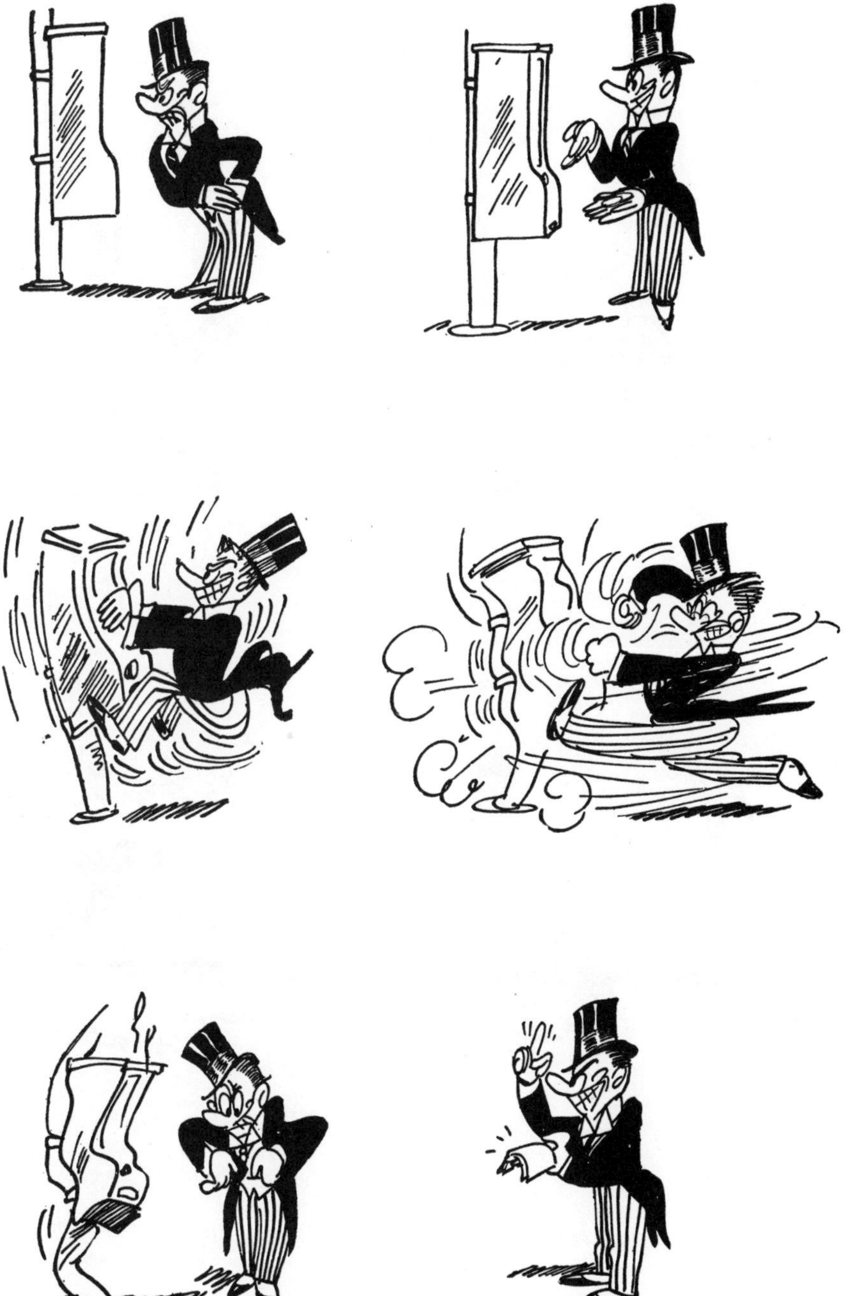

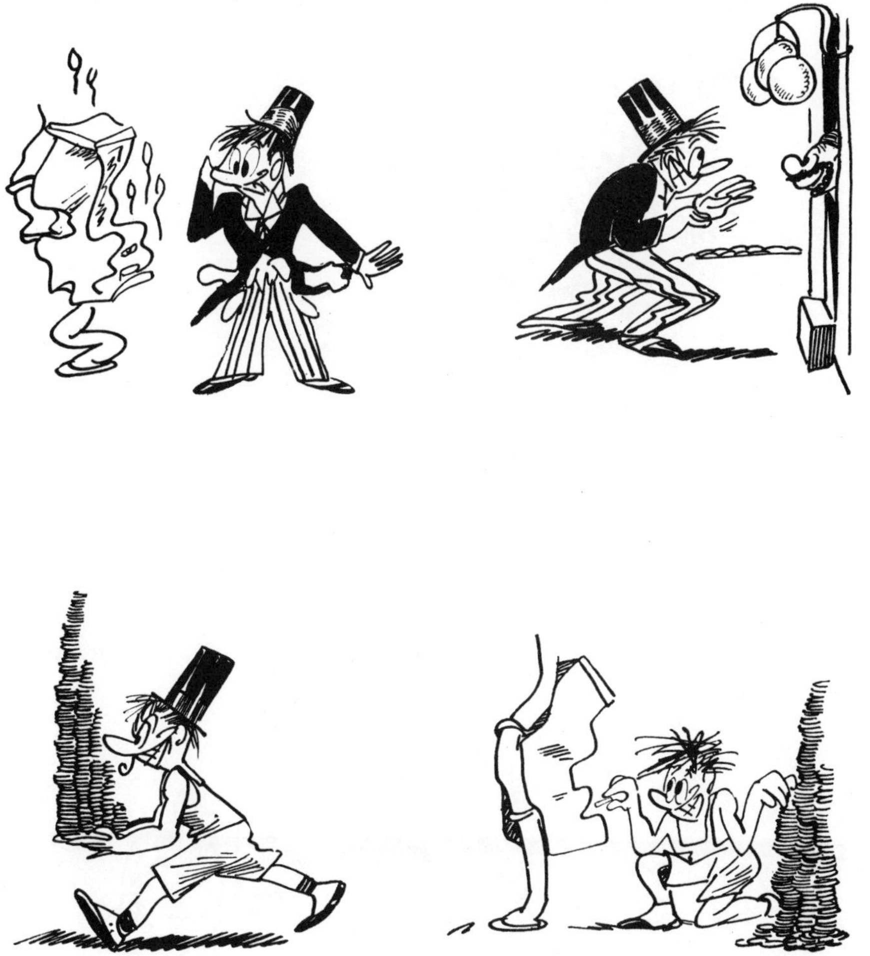

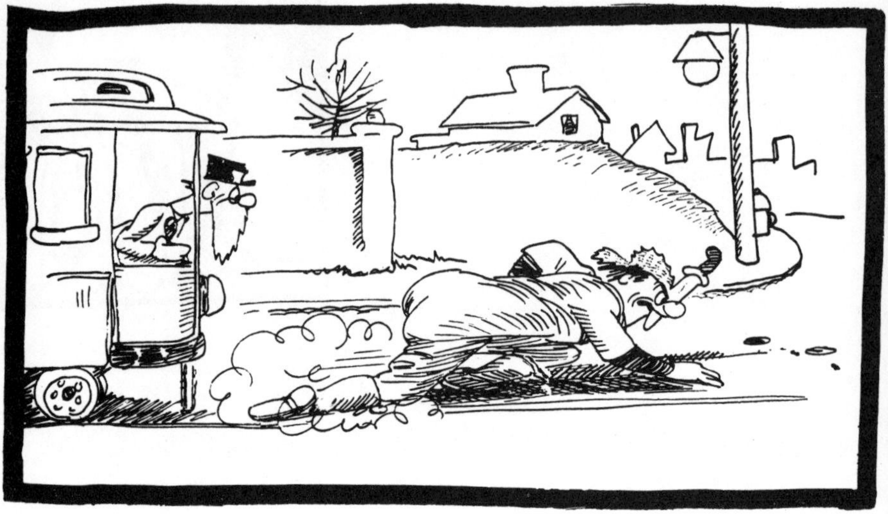

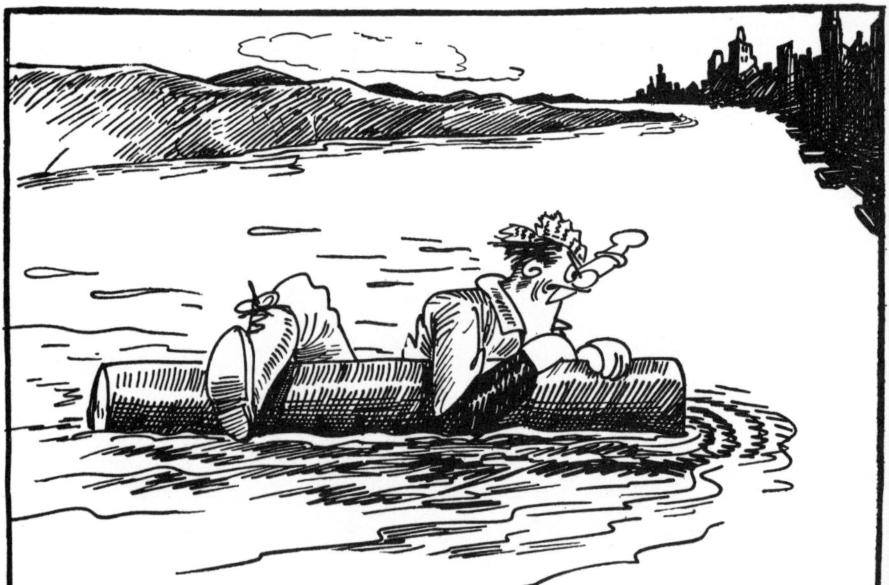

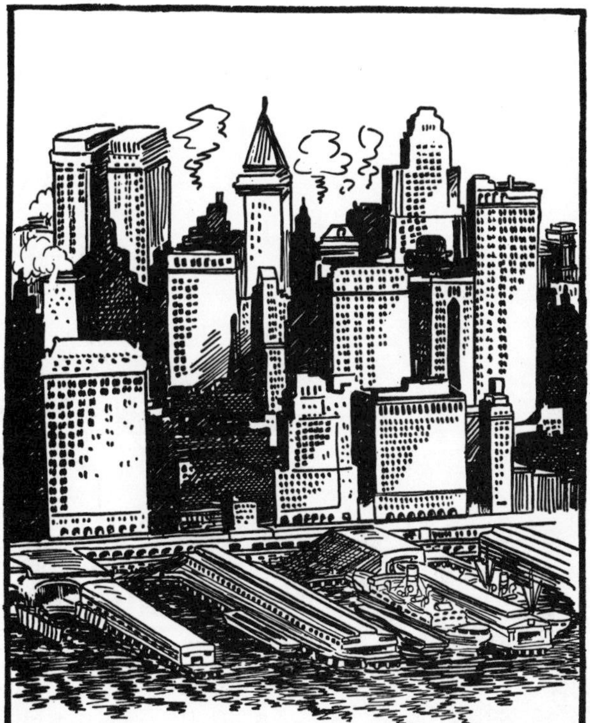
NEW JERSEY

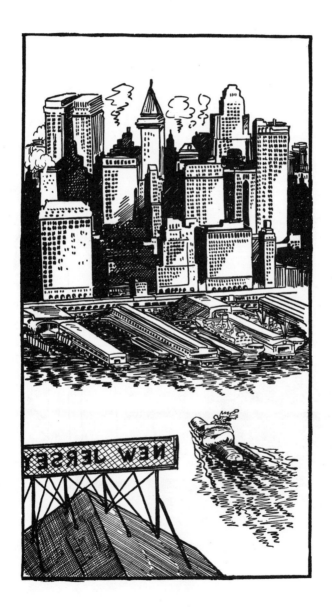

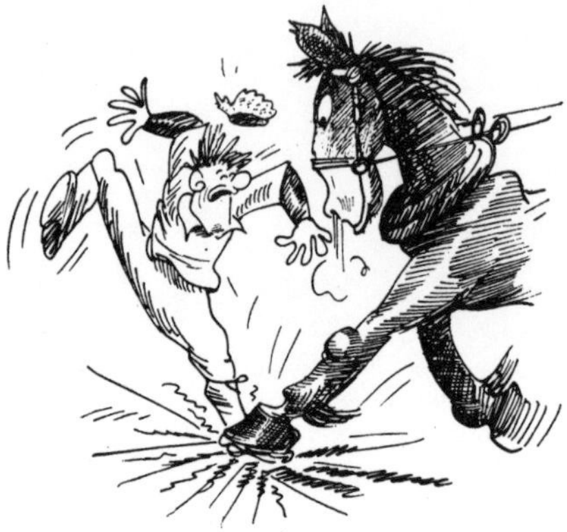

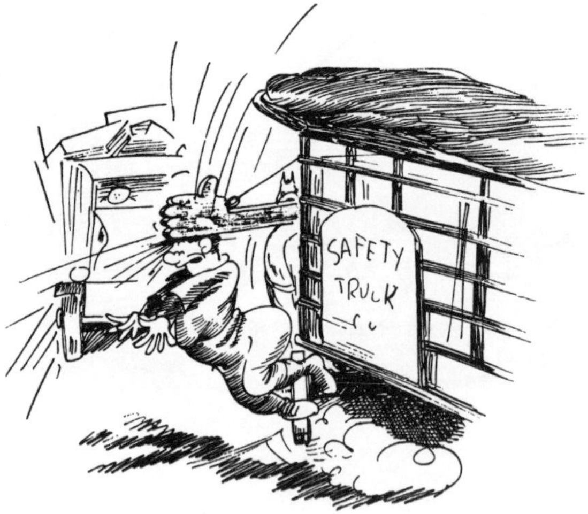
SAFETY
TRUCK

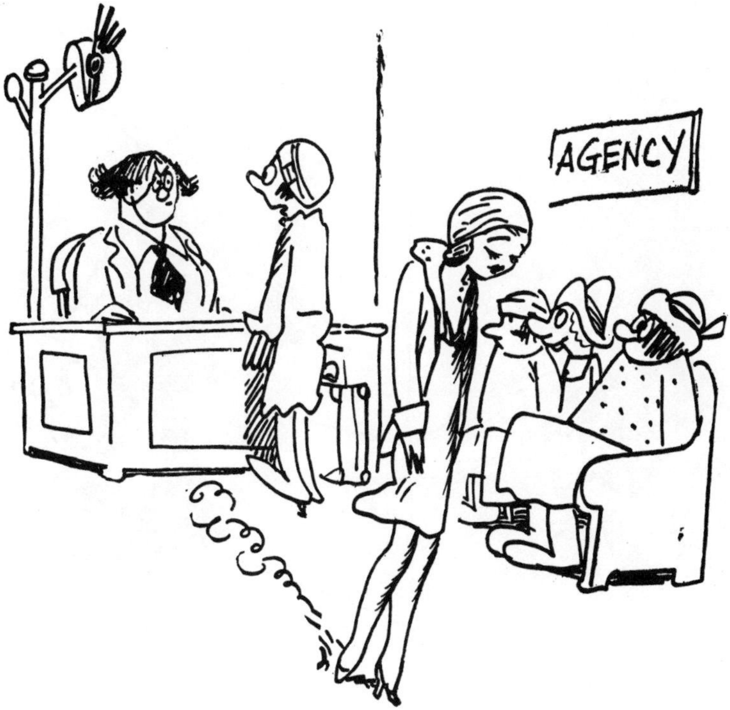
AGENCY

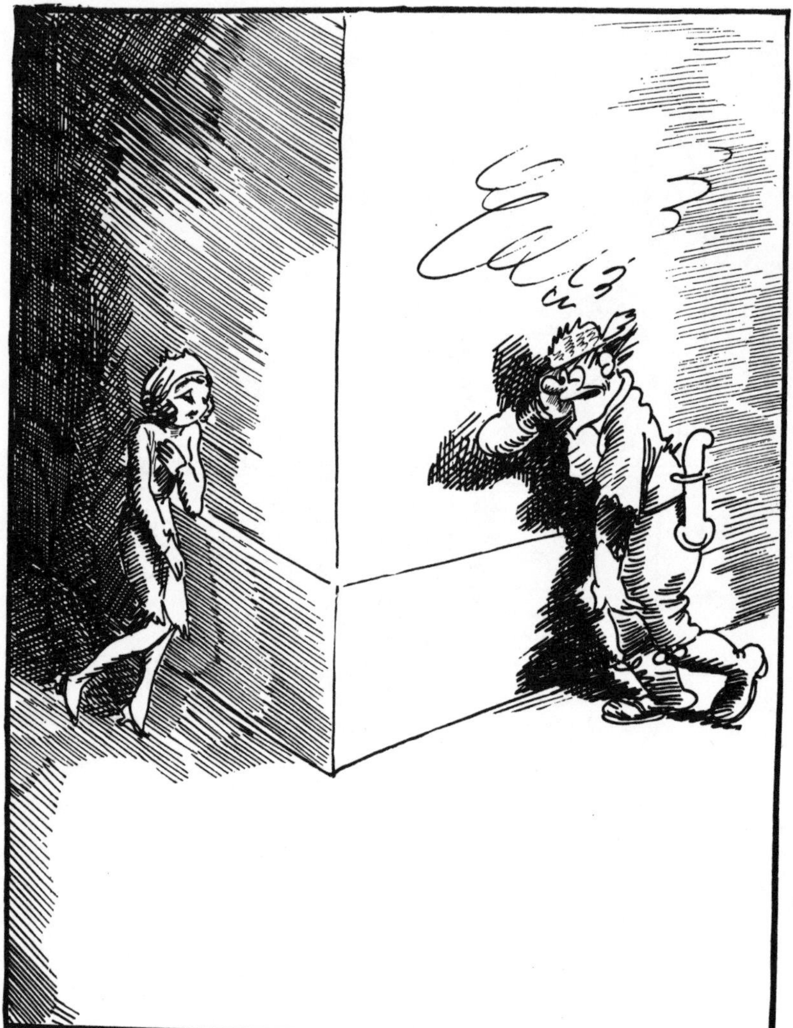

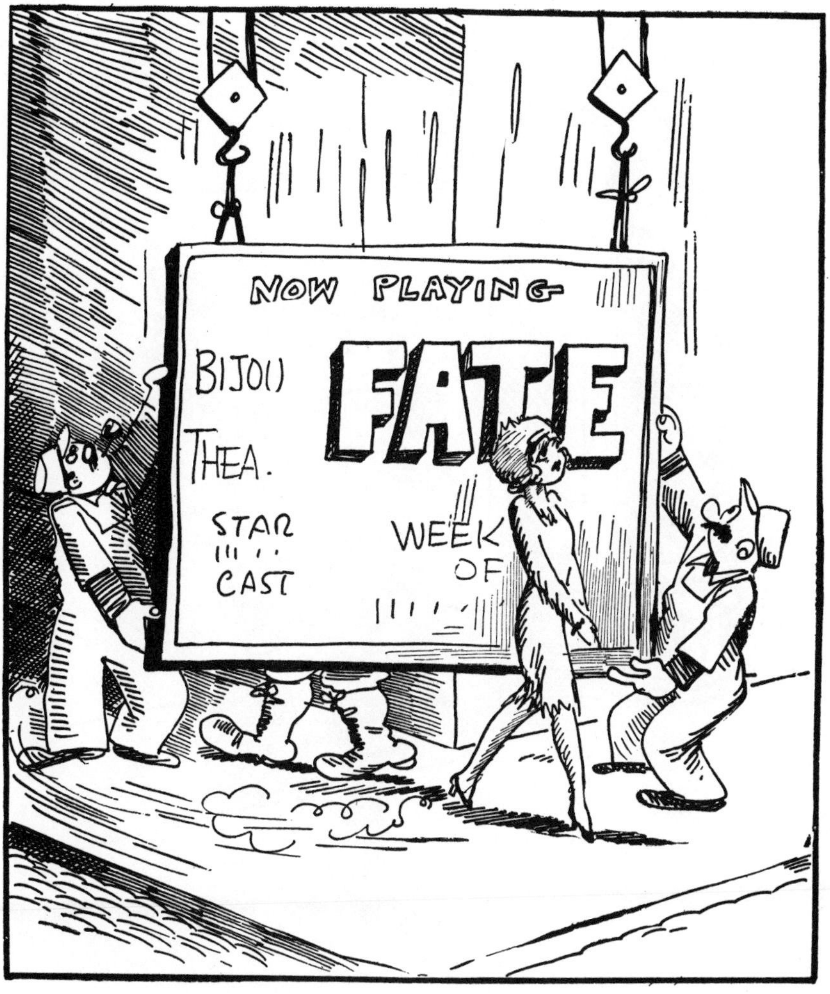
NOW PLAYING
BIJOU
THEA.
FATE
STAR
CAST
WEEK
OF

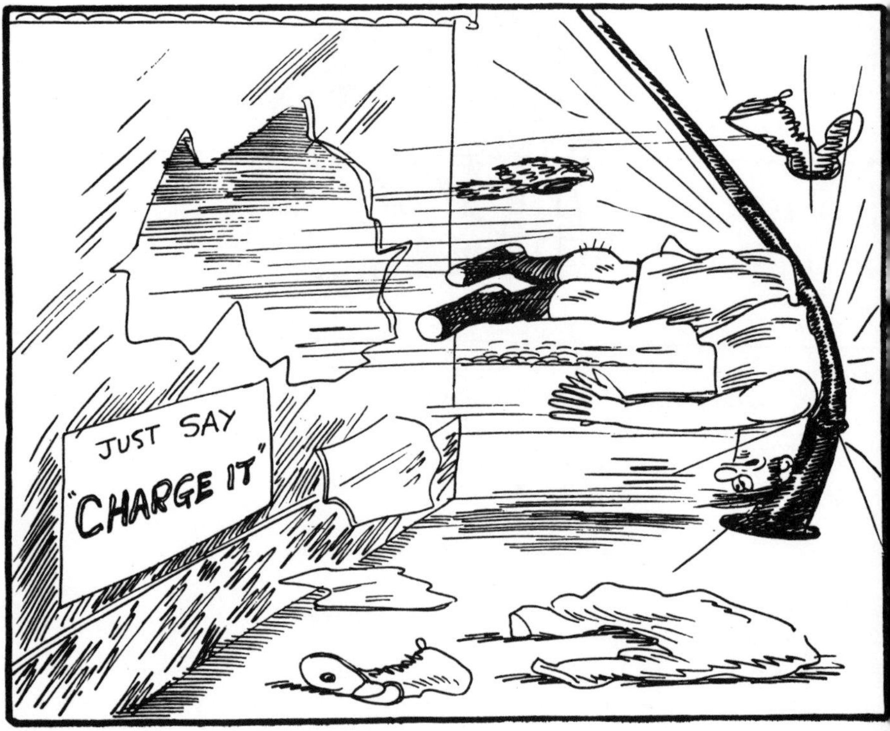
JUST SAY
"CHARGE IT"

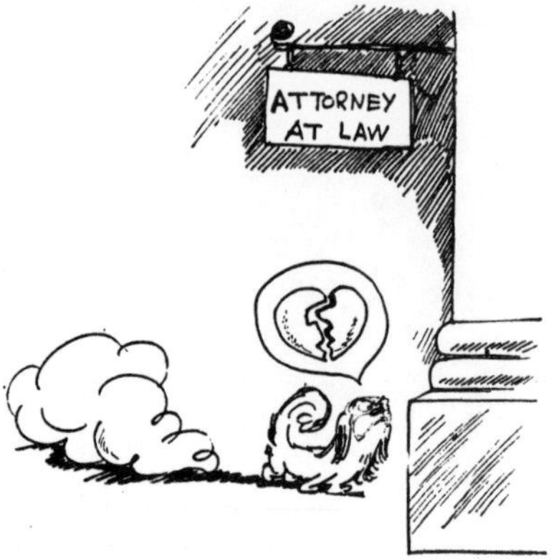
ATTORNEY
AT LAW

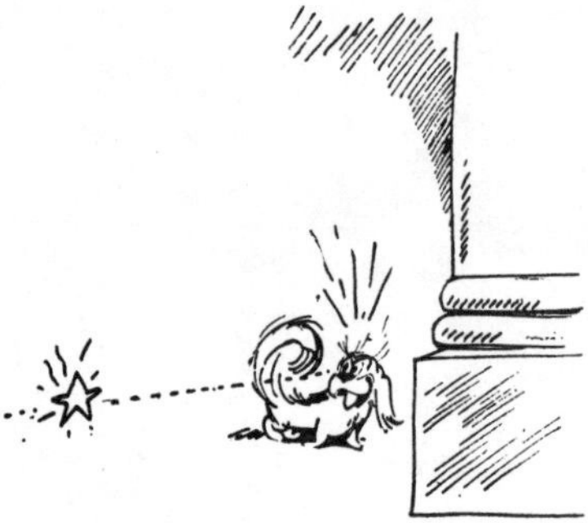

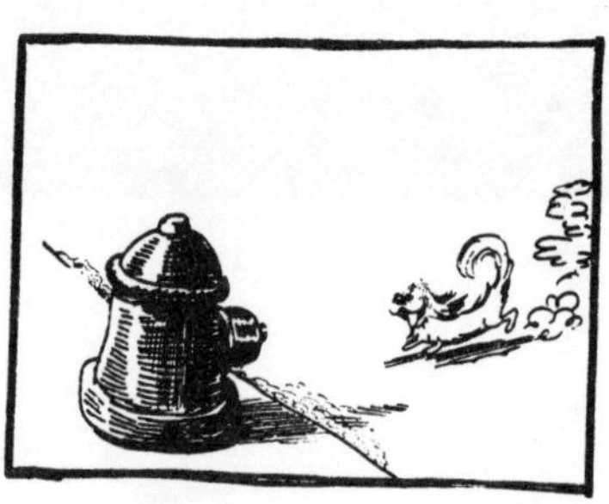

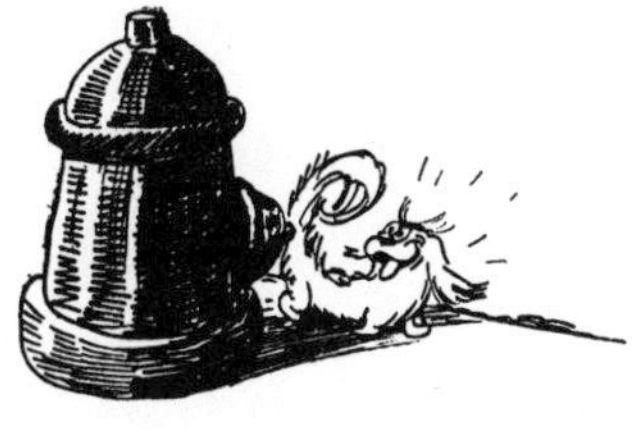

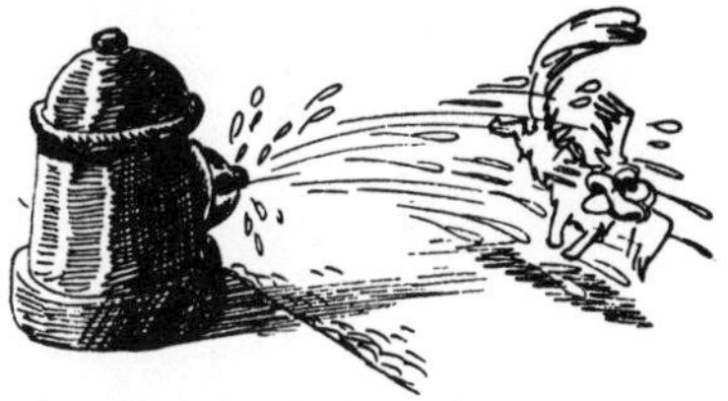

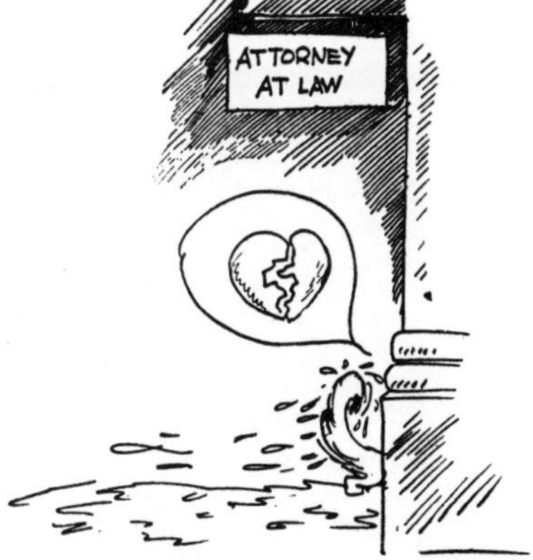
ATTORNEY
AT LAW

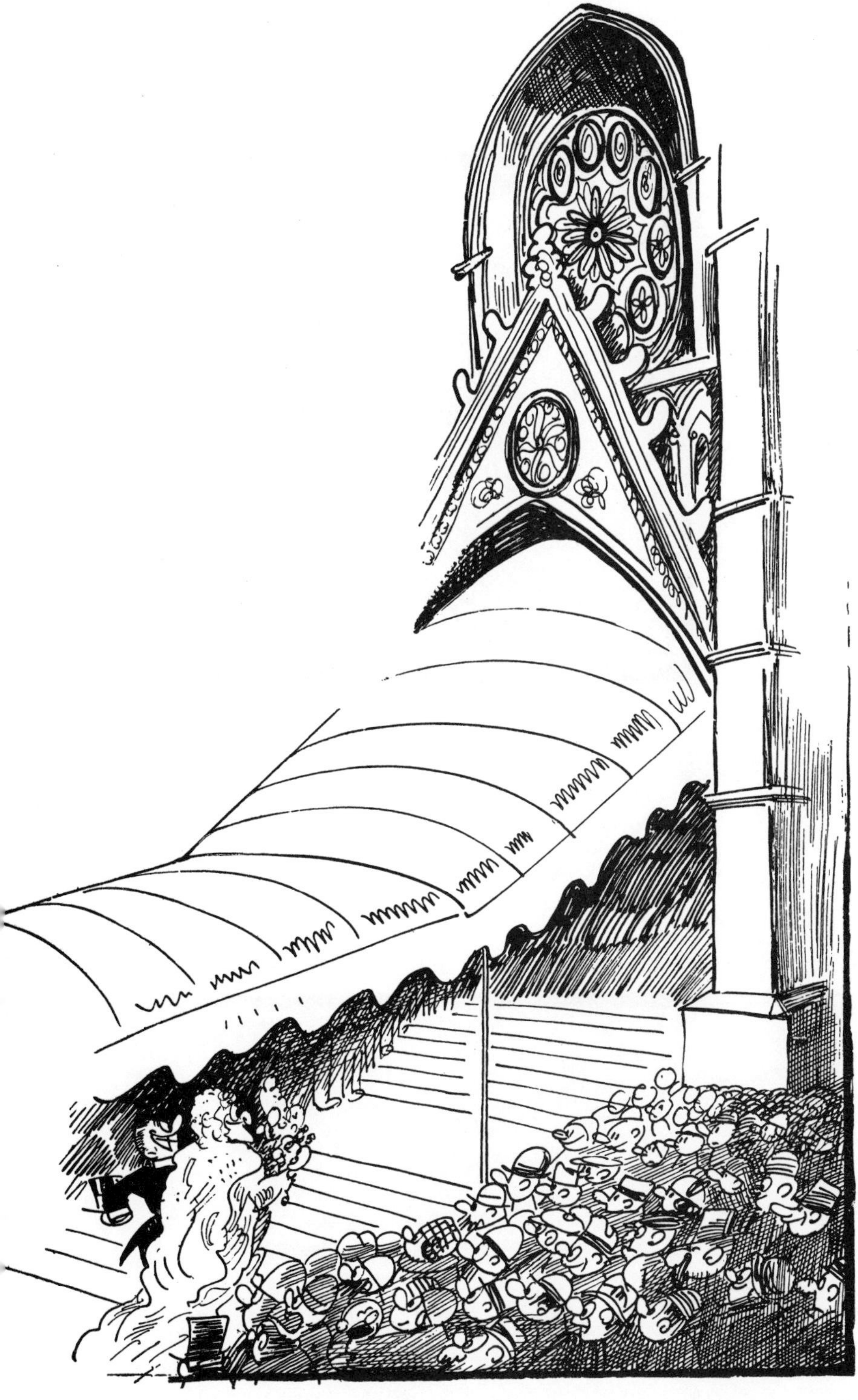

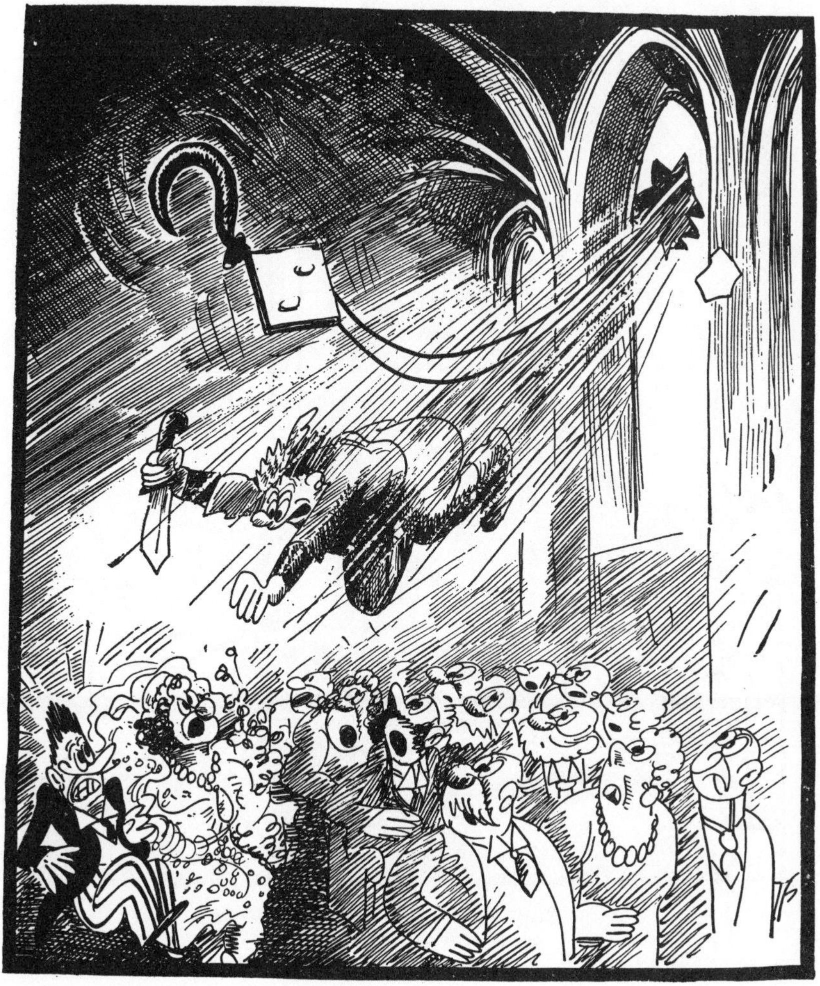

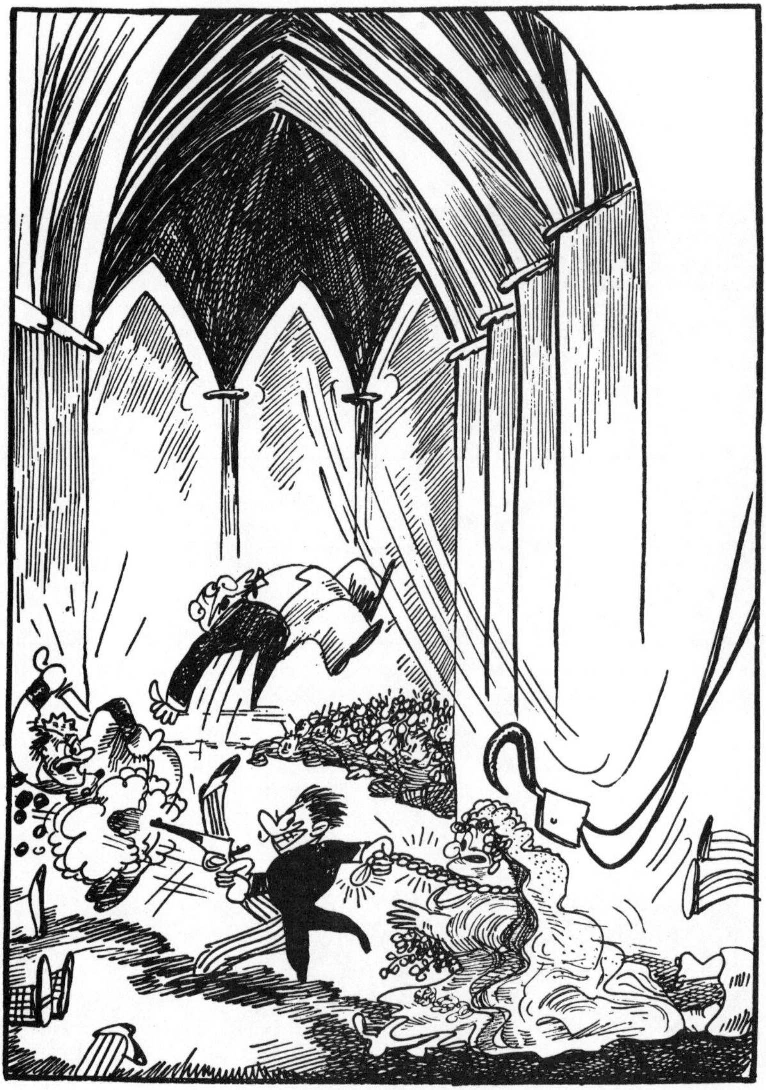

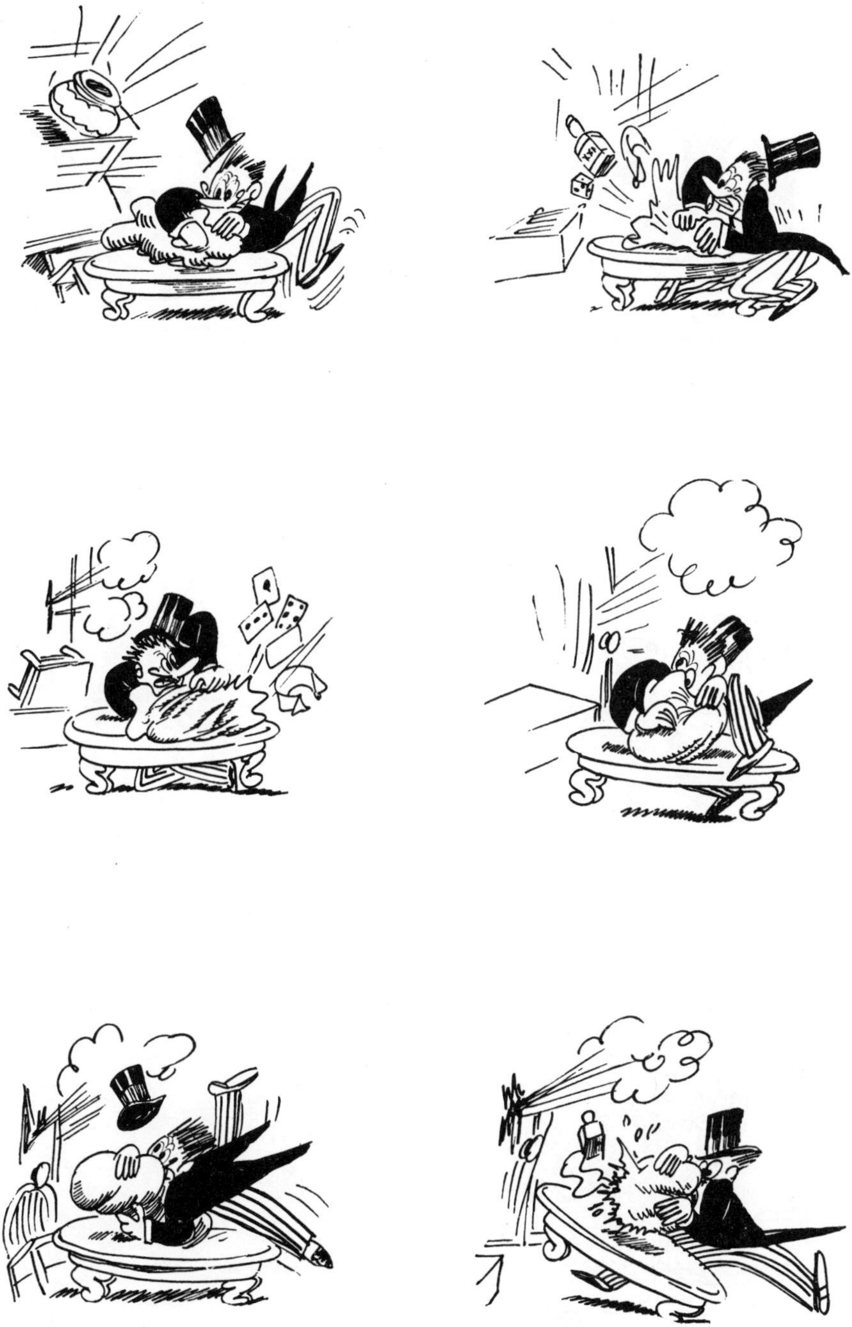

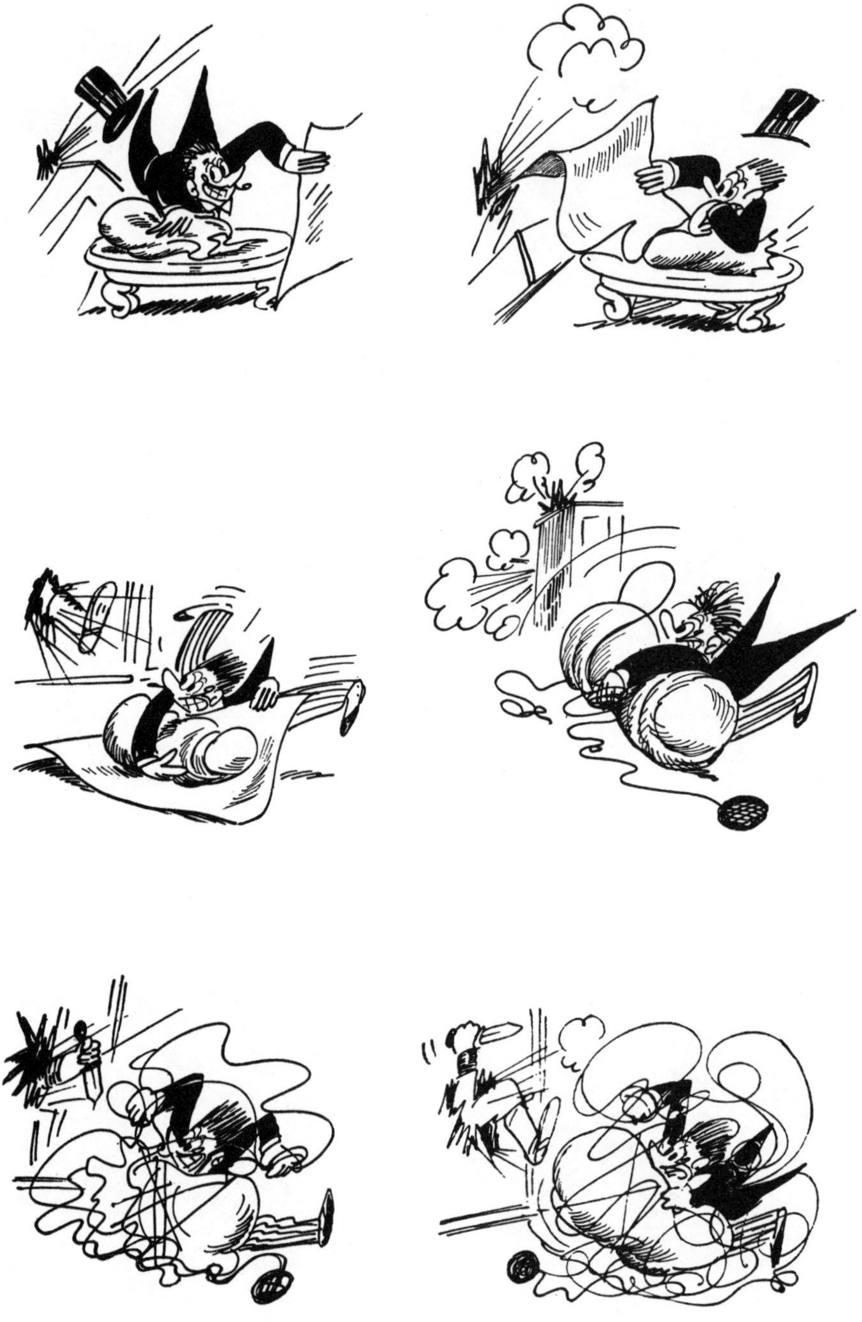

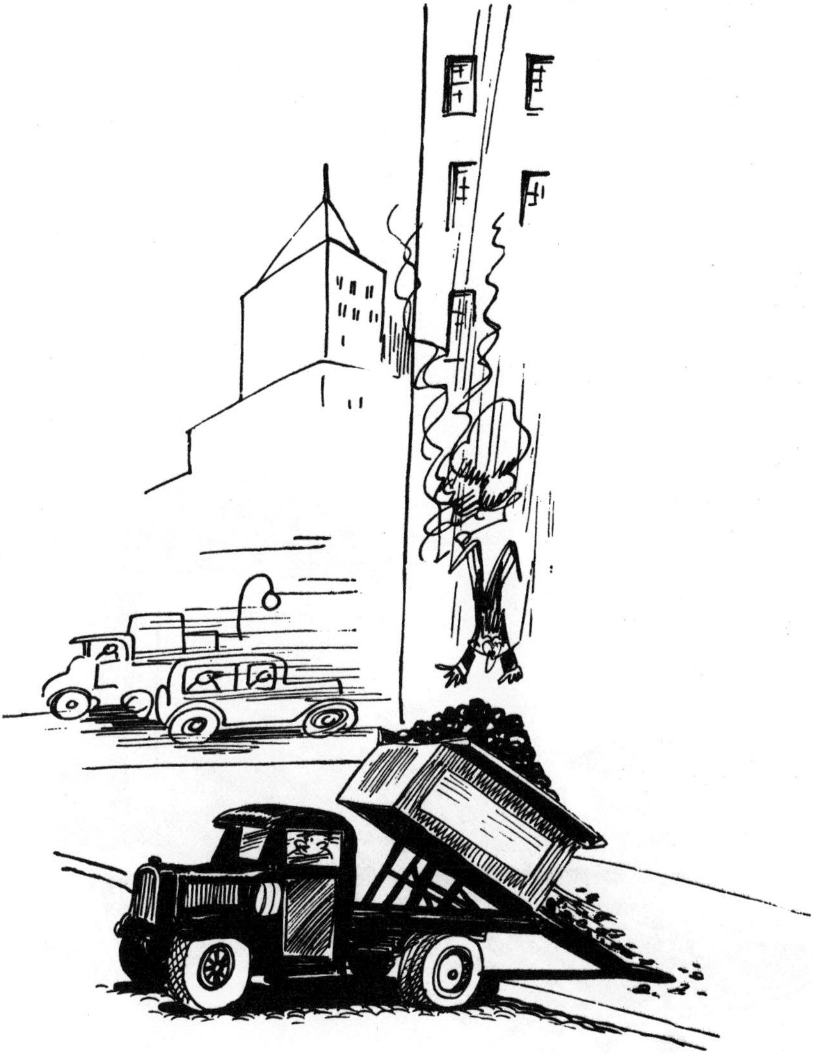

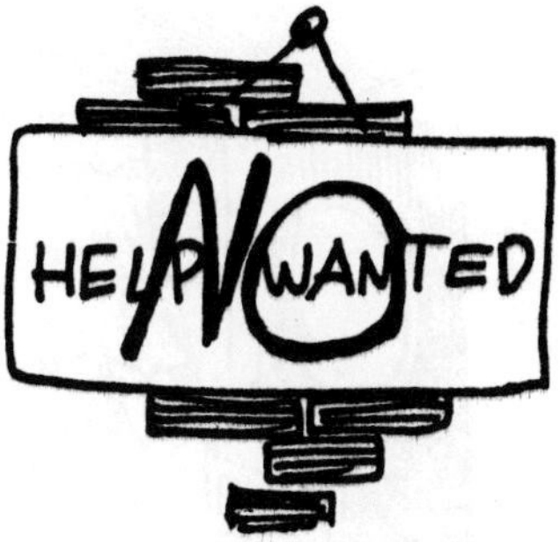

HELP WANTED
NO

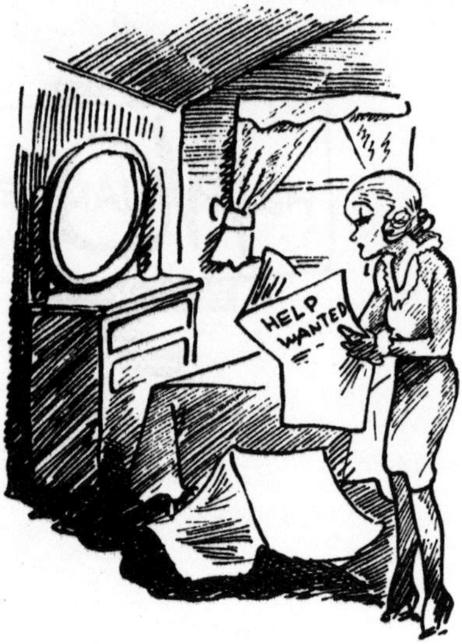
HELP WANTED

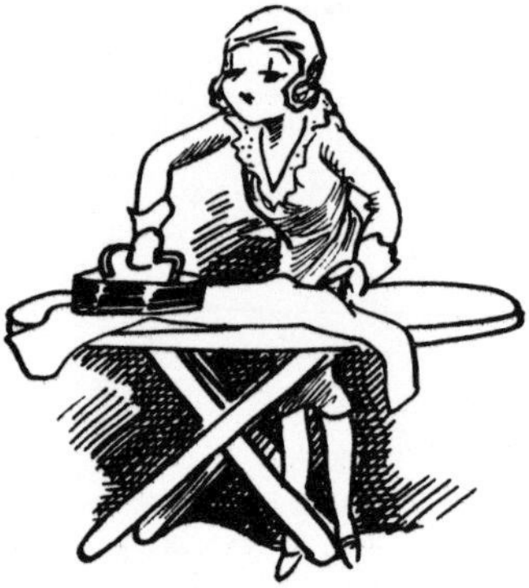

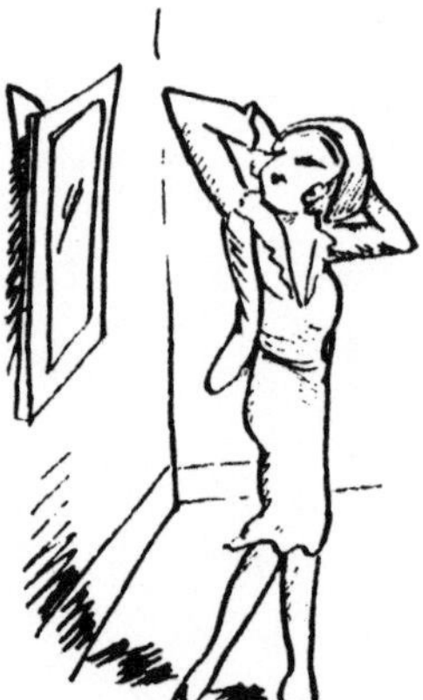

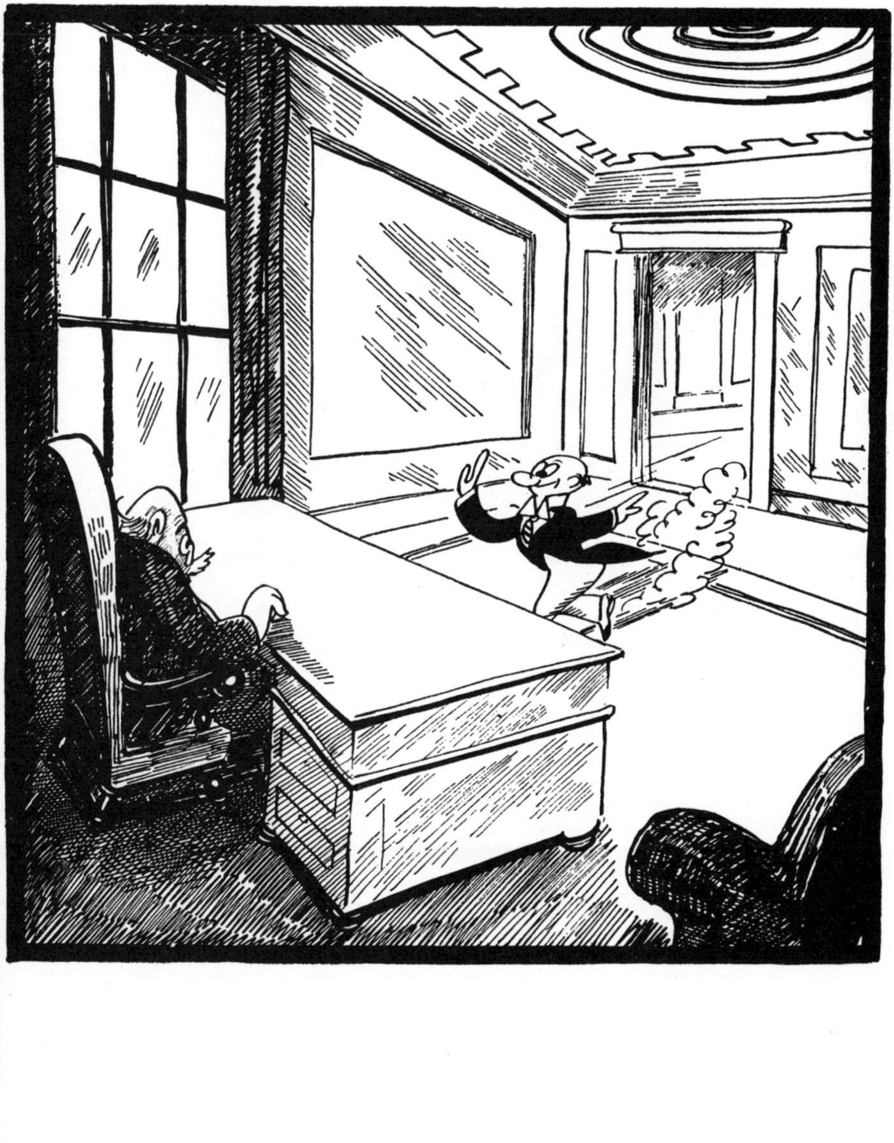

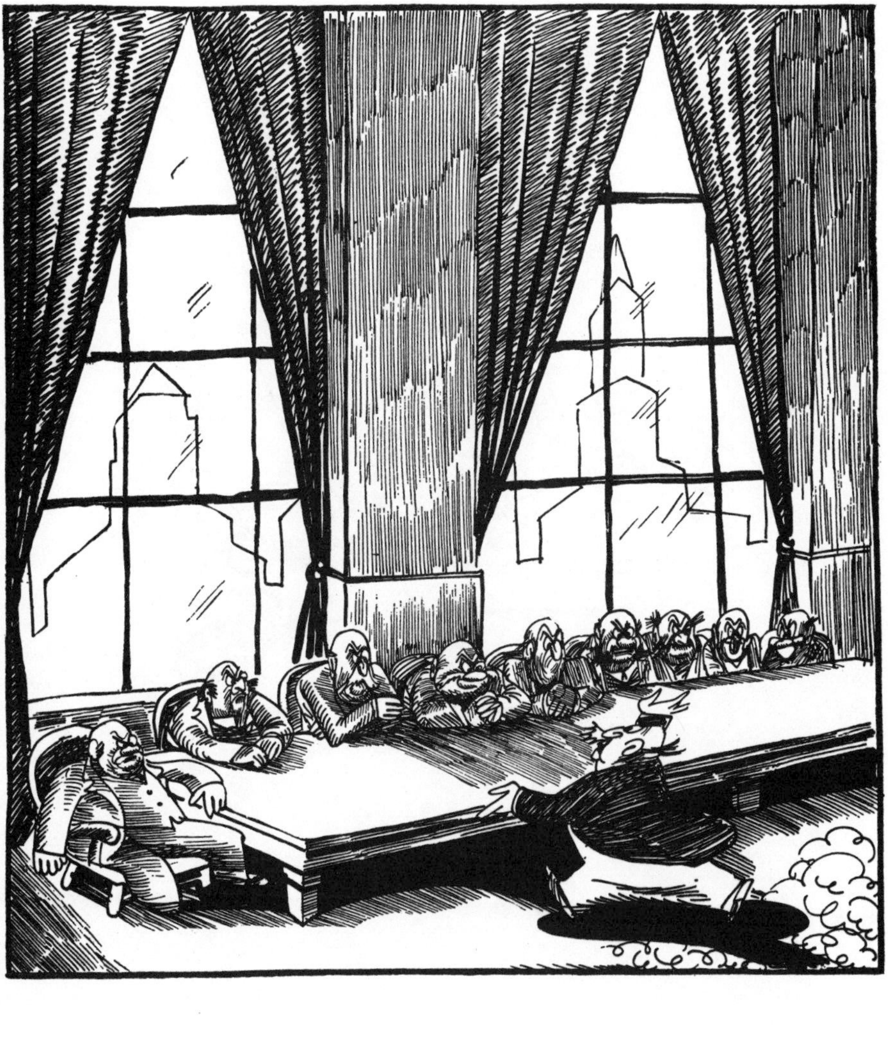

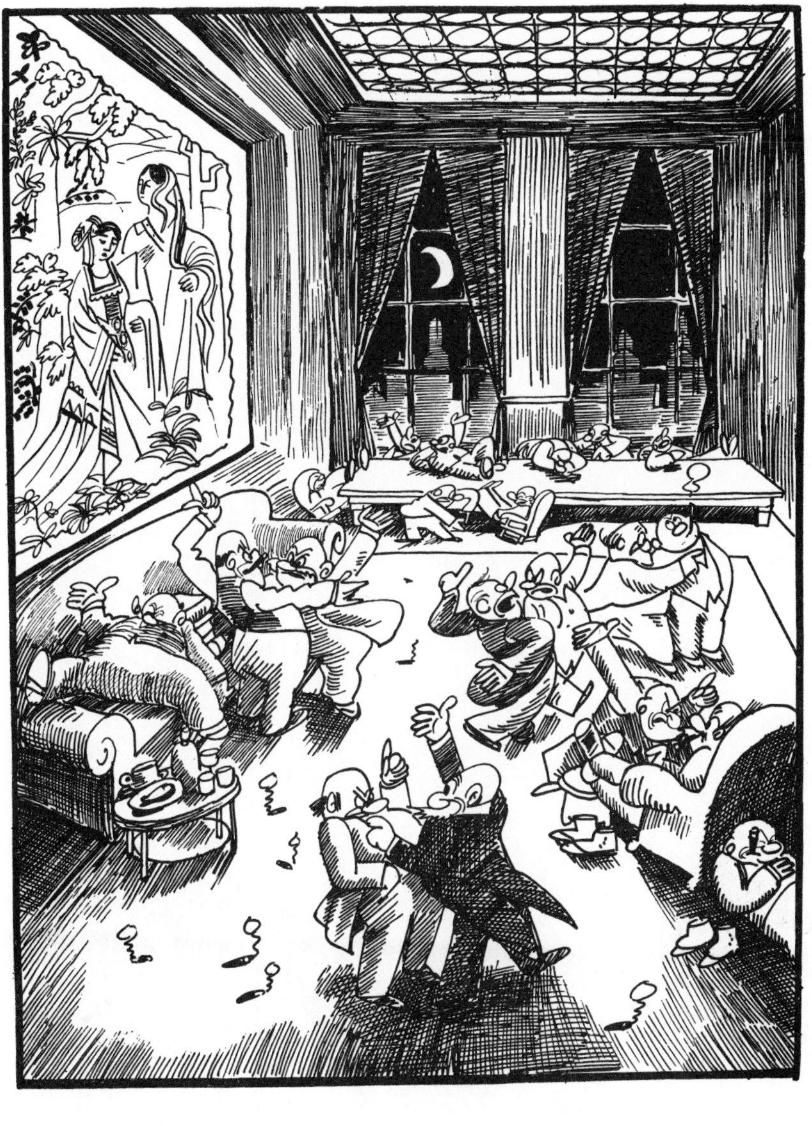

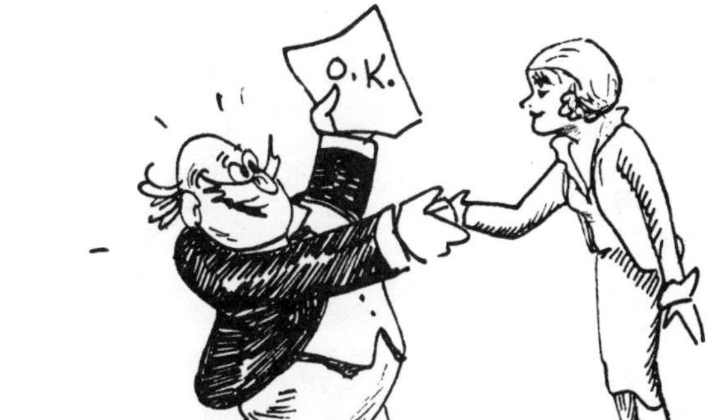
O.K.

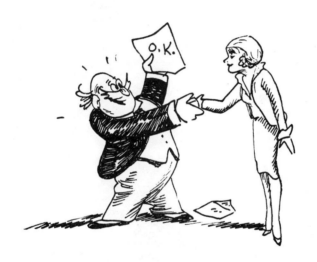

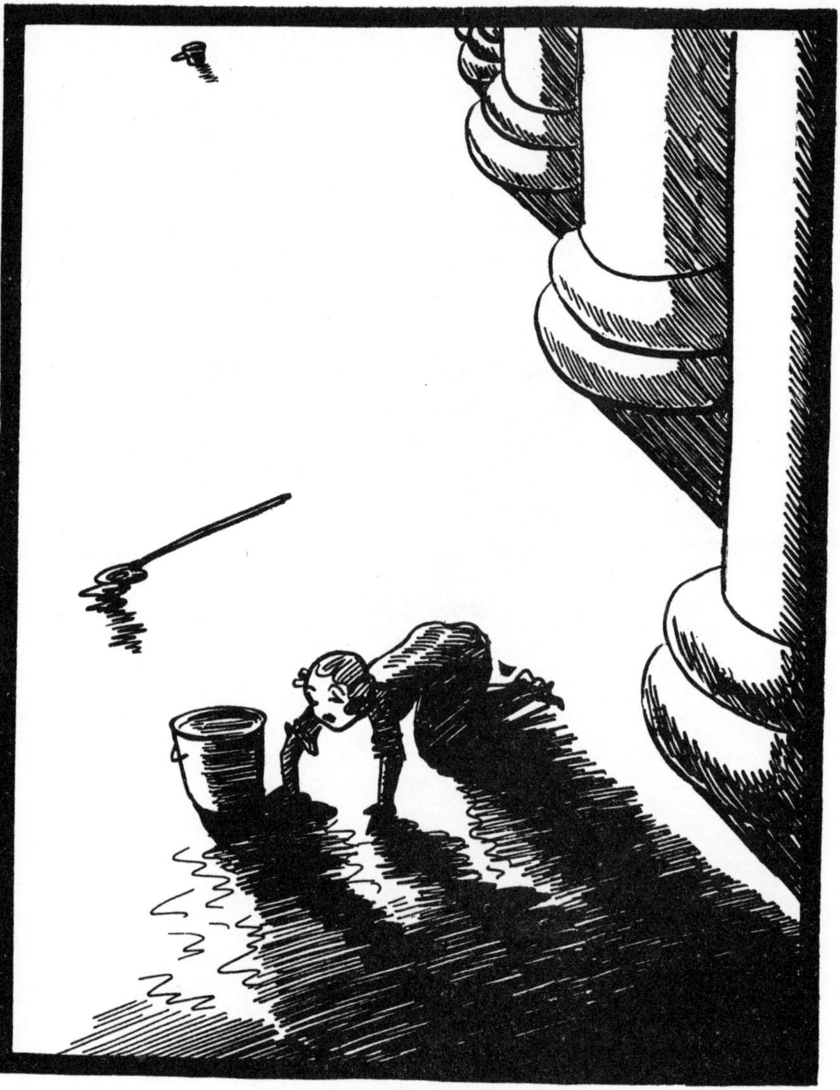

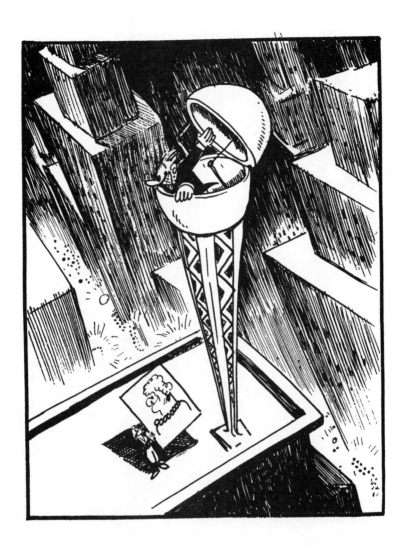

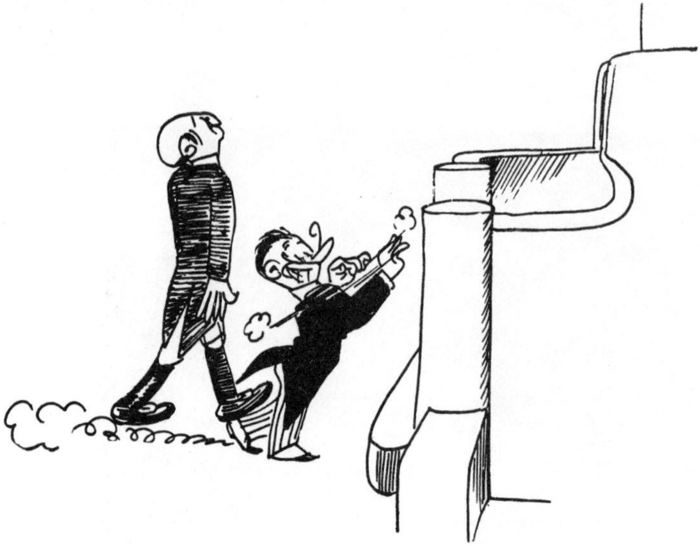

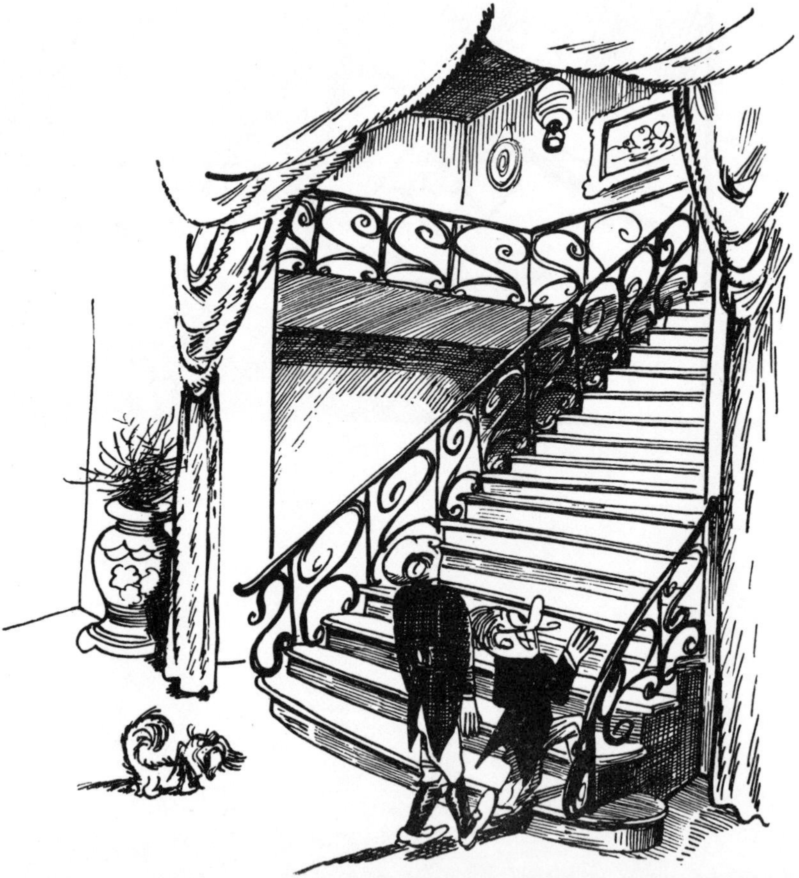

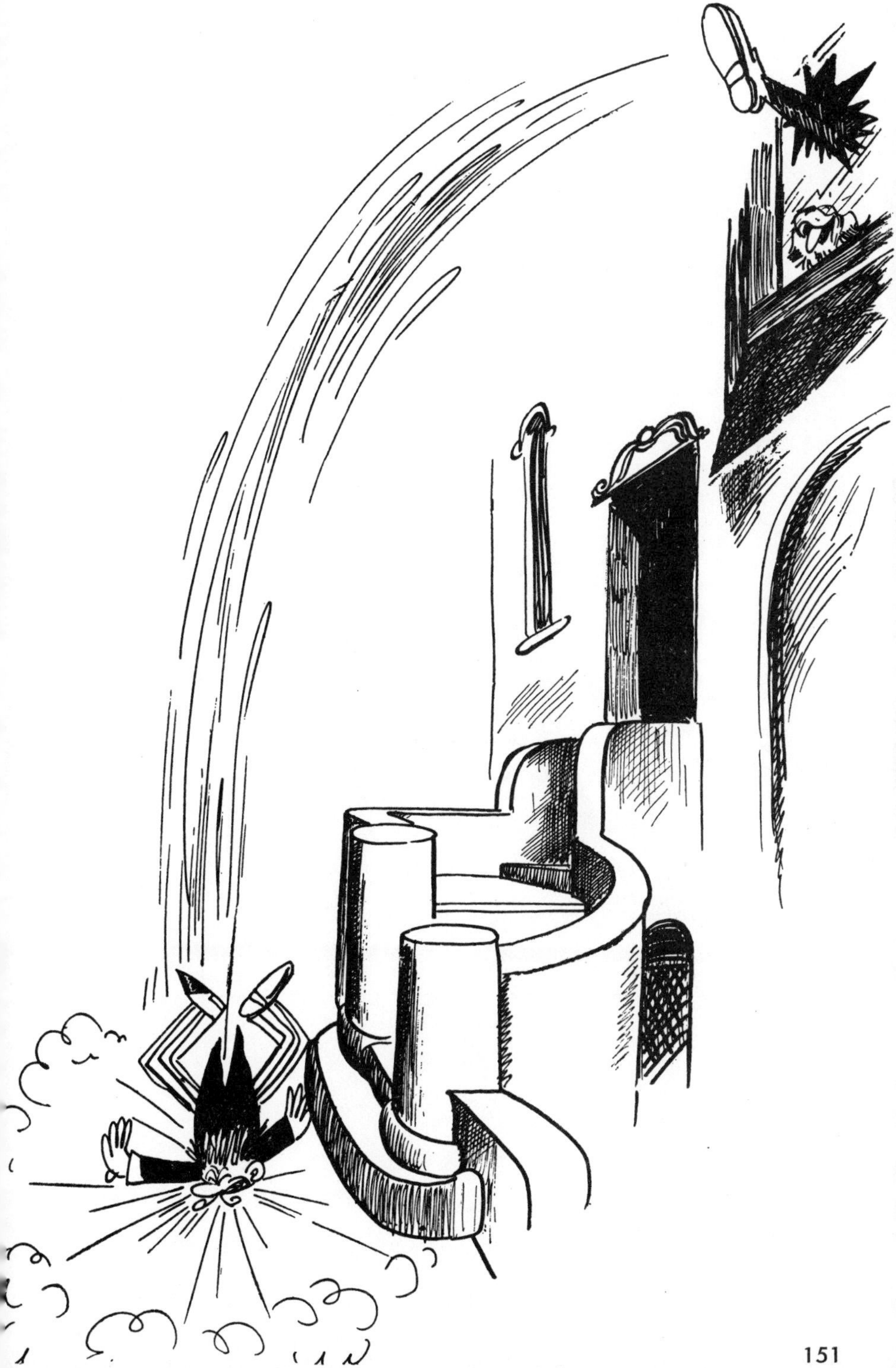

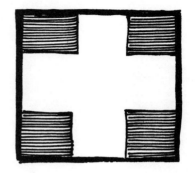

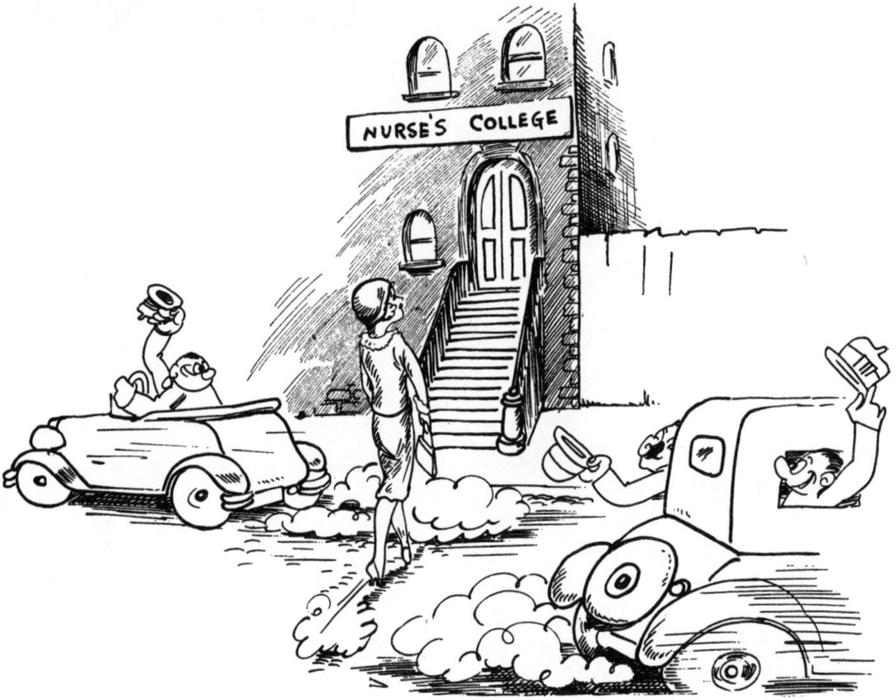
NURSE'S COLLEGE

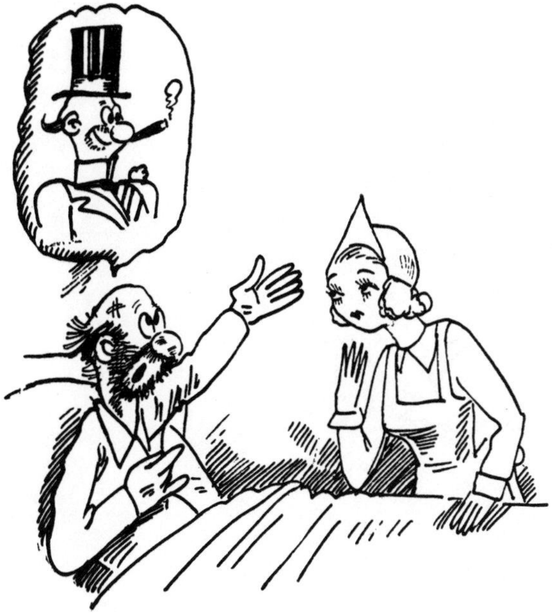

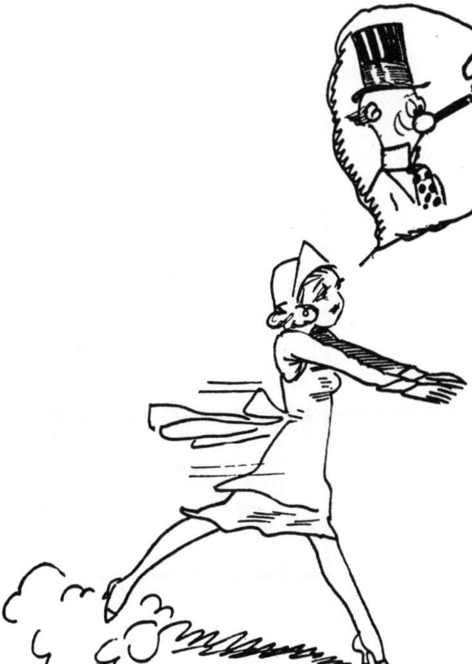

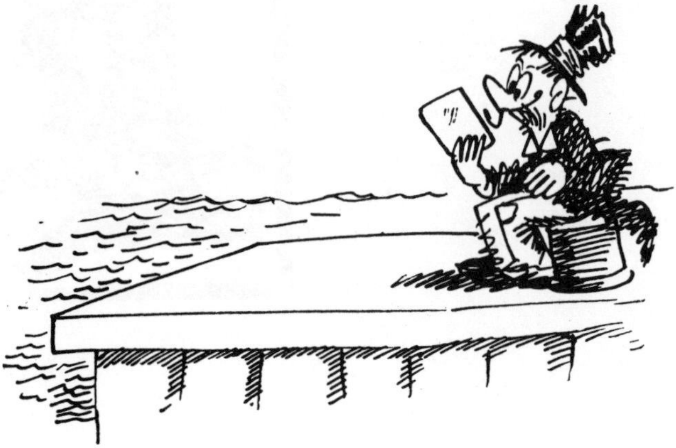

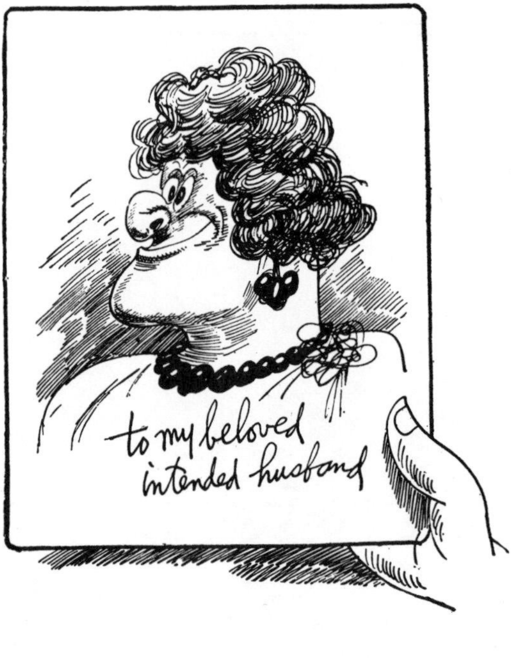
to my beloved
intended husband

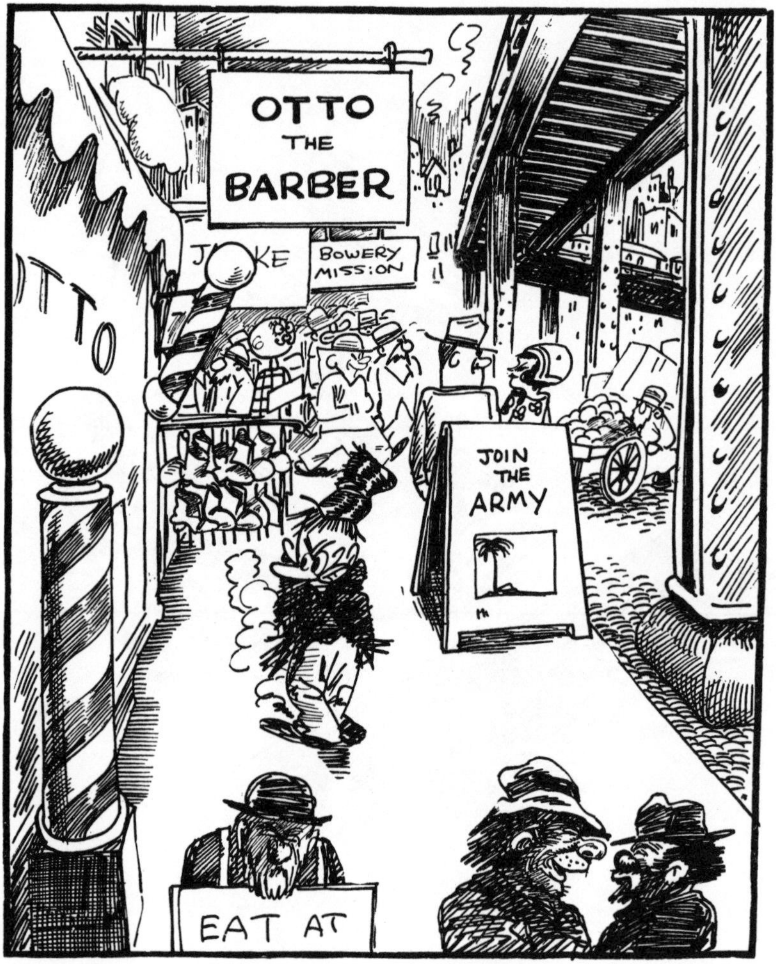
OTTO
THE
BARBER
BOWERY
MISSION
OTTO
JOIN
THE
ARMY
EAT AT

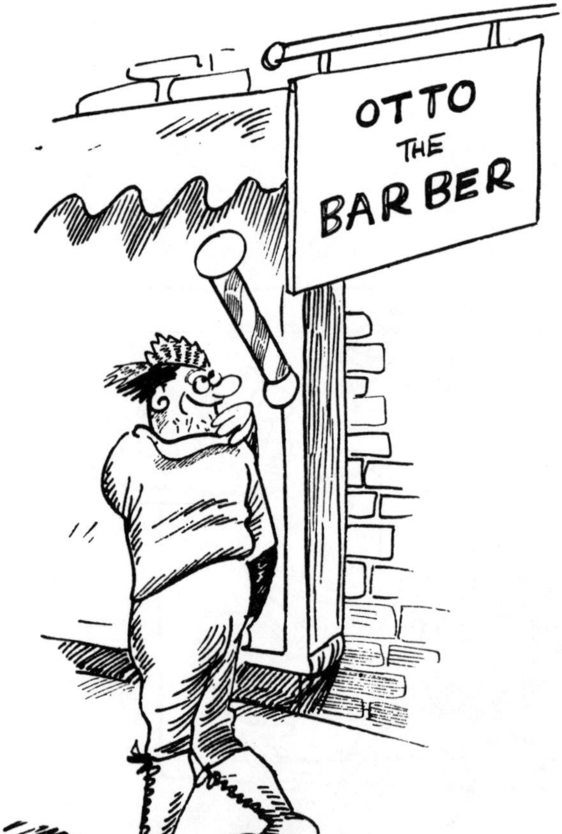
OTTO
THE
BARBER

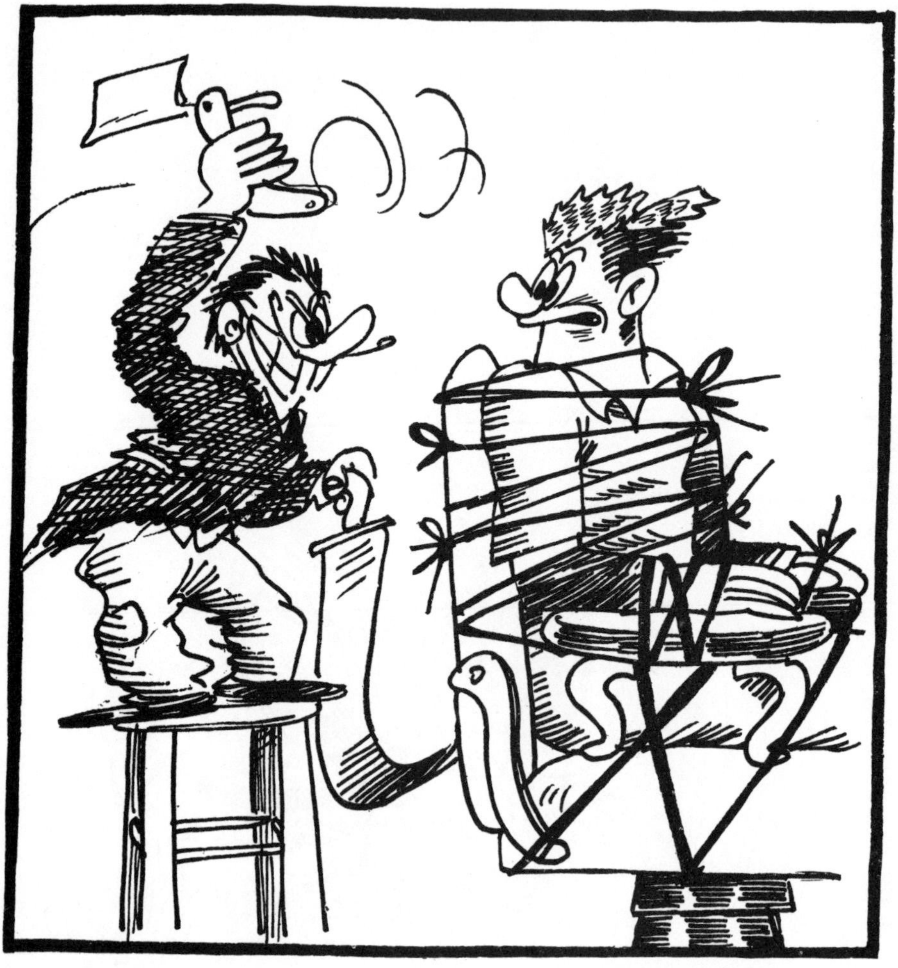

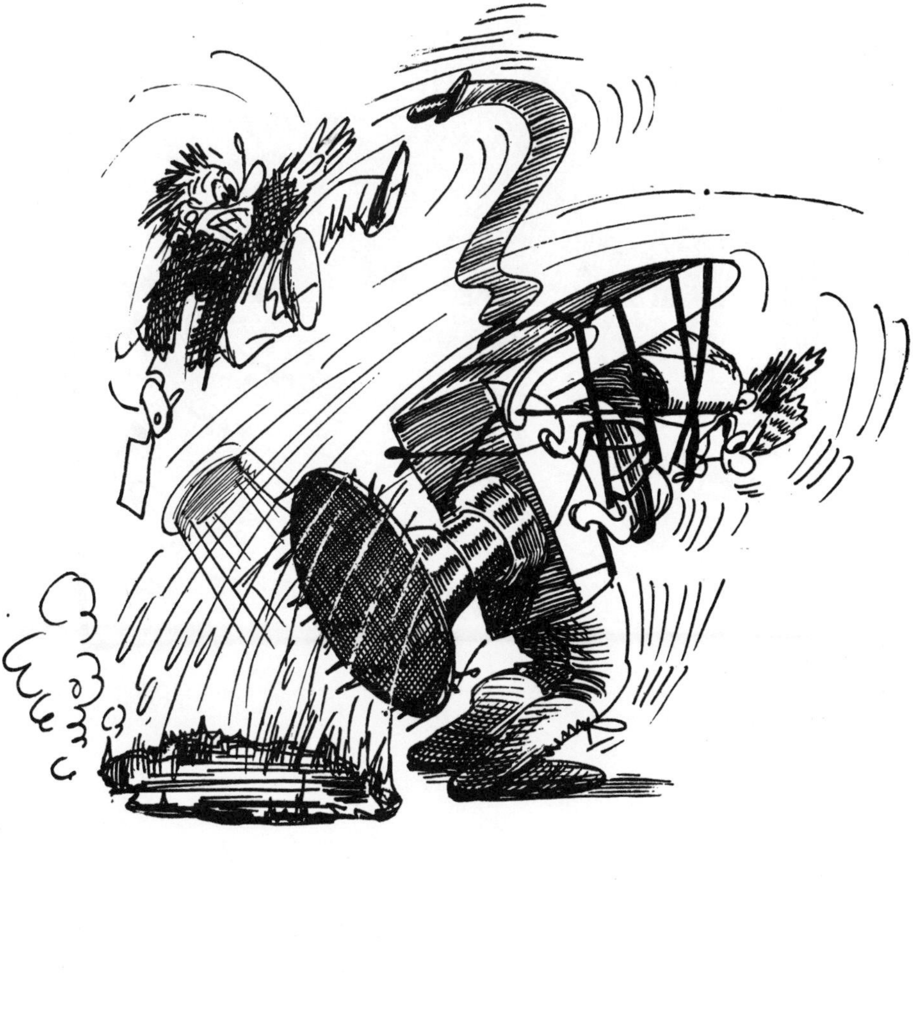

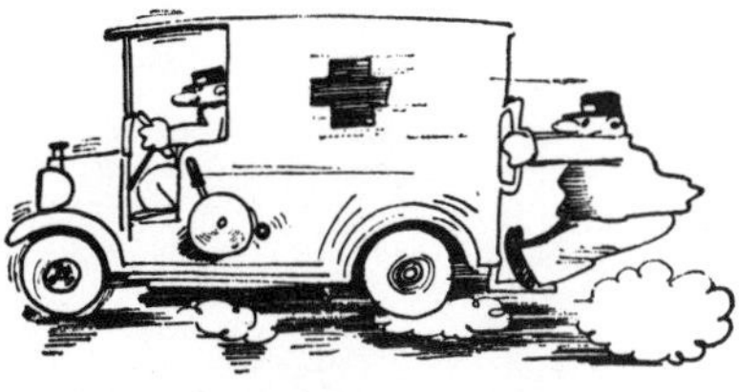

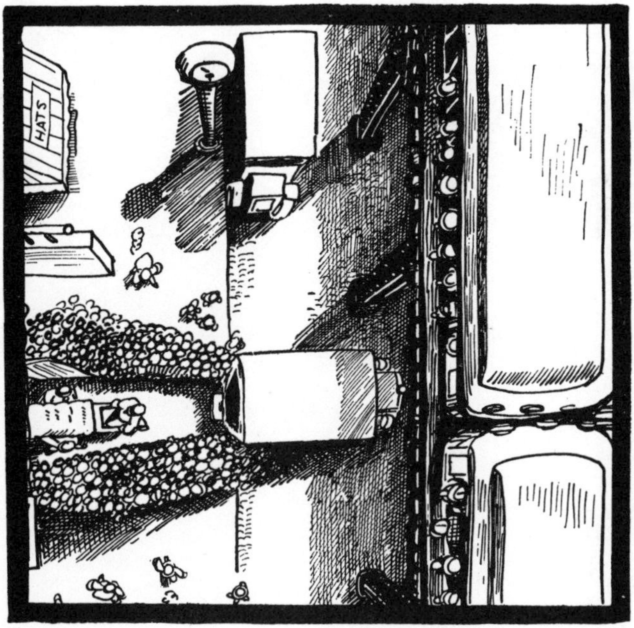
HATS

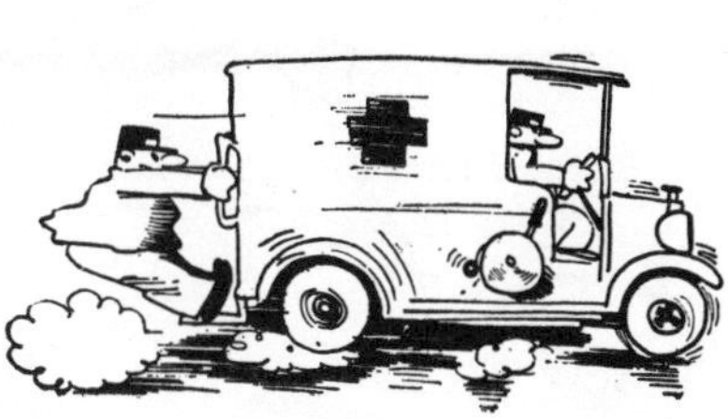

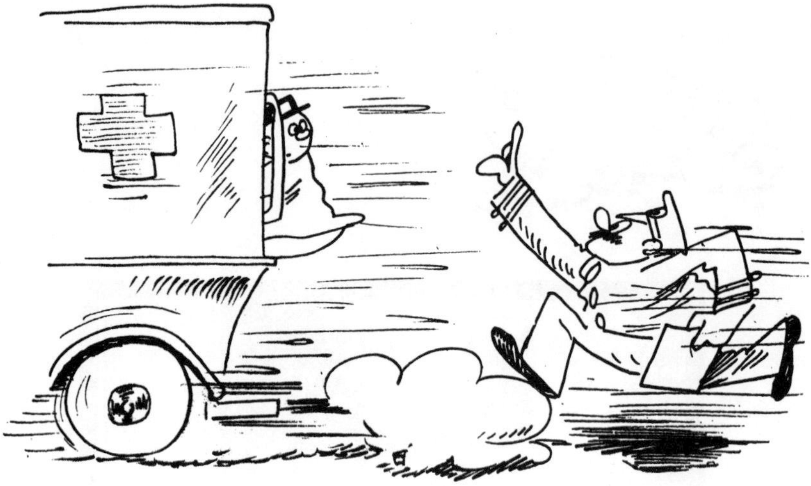

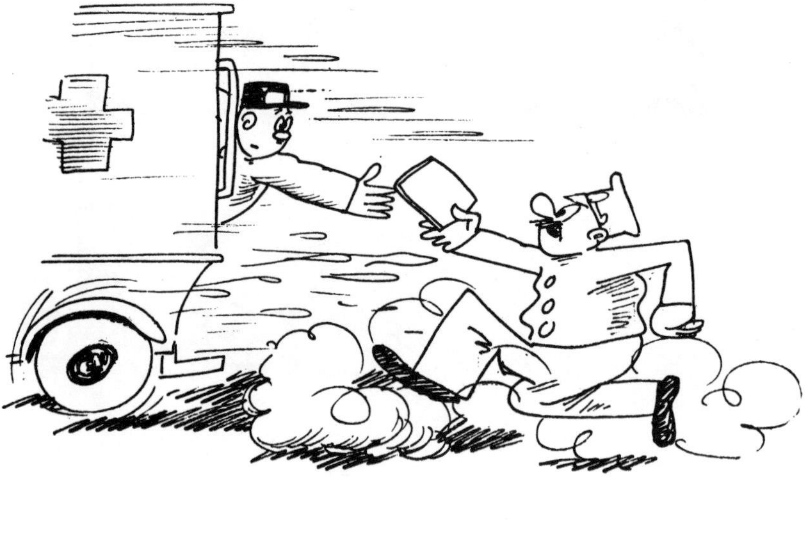

to my beloved
intended husband

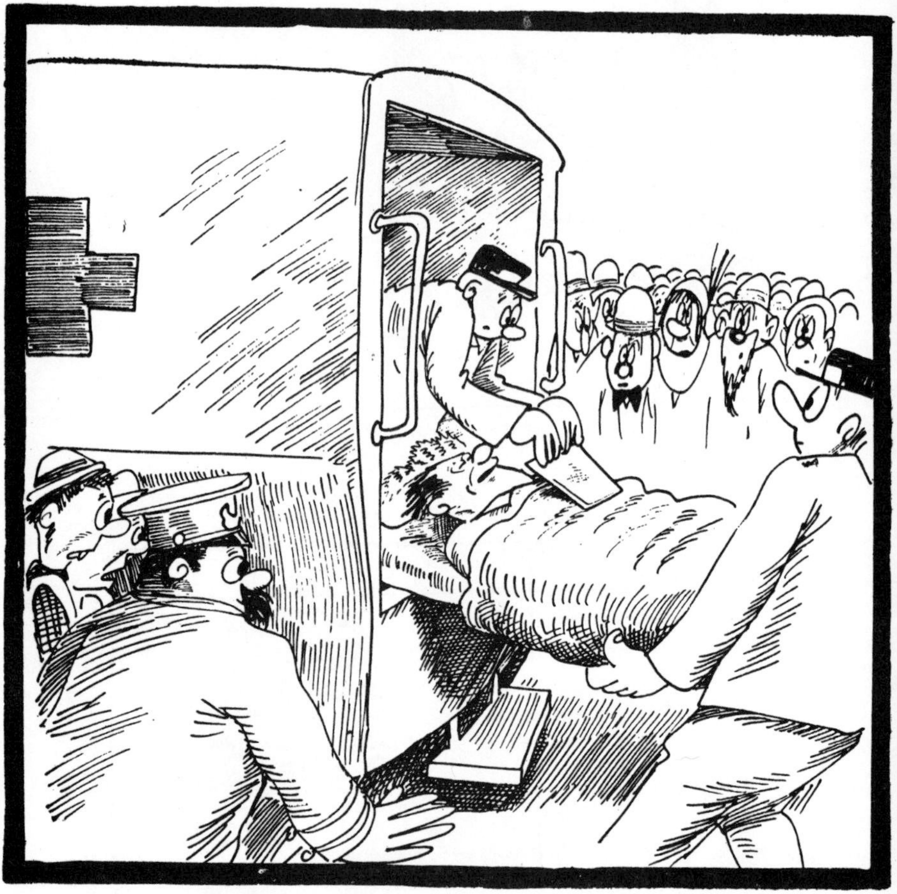

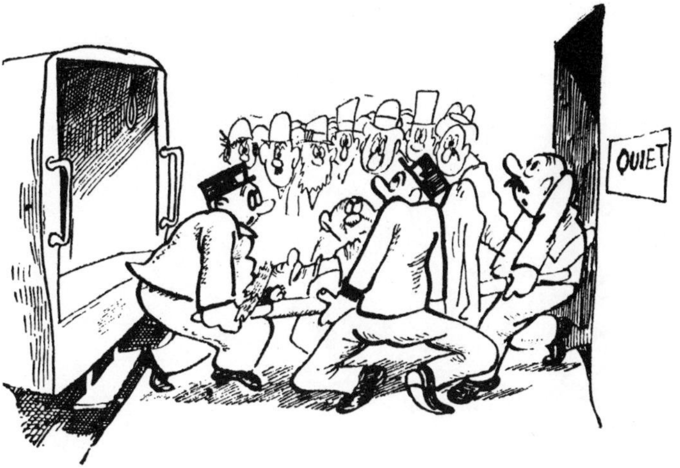
QUIET

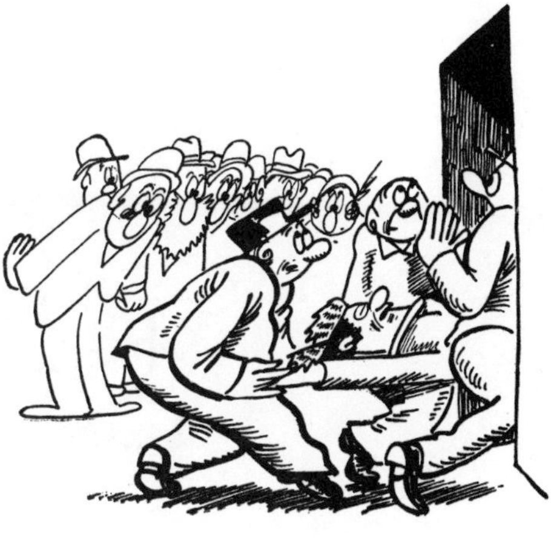

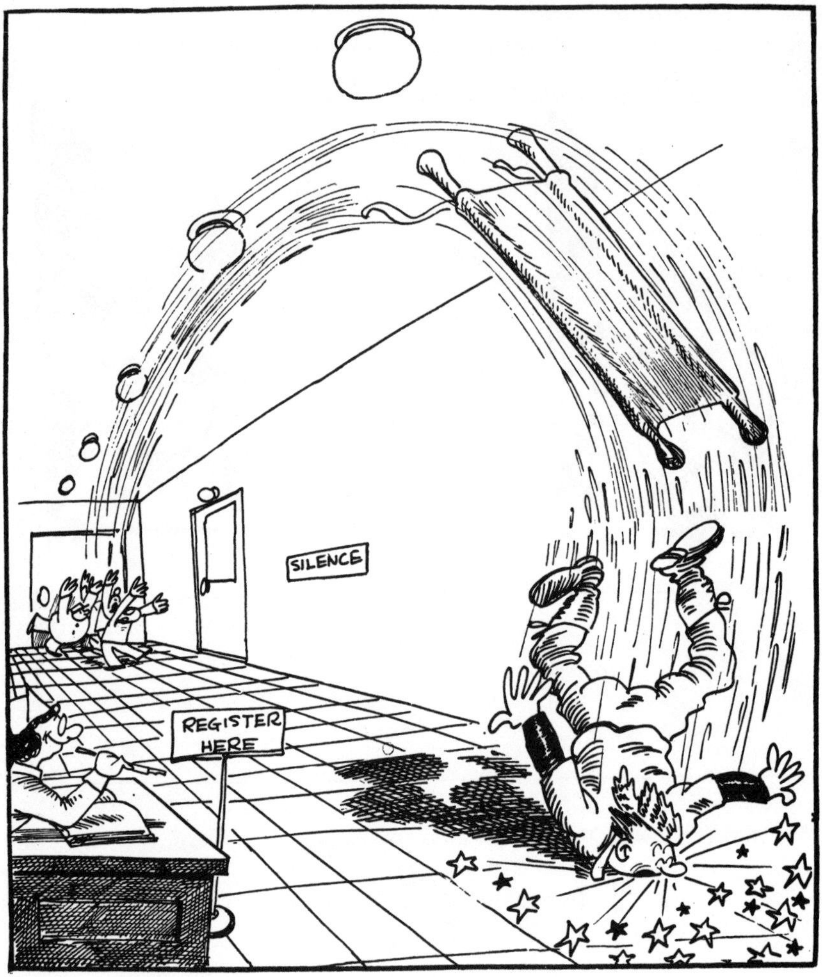
SILENCE
REGISTER HERE

to my beloved
intended husband

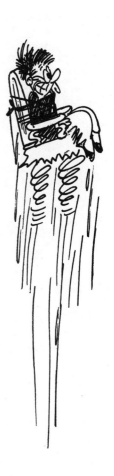

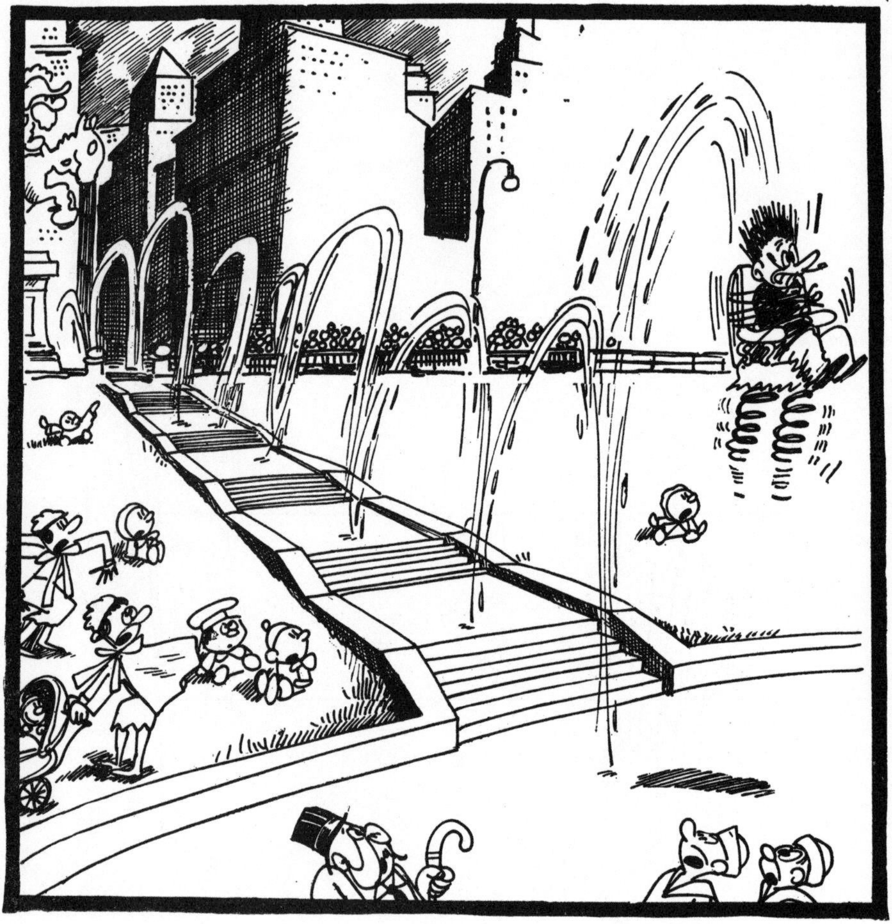

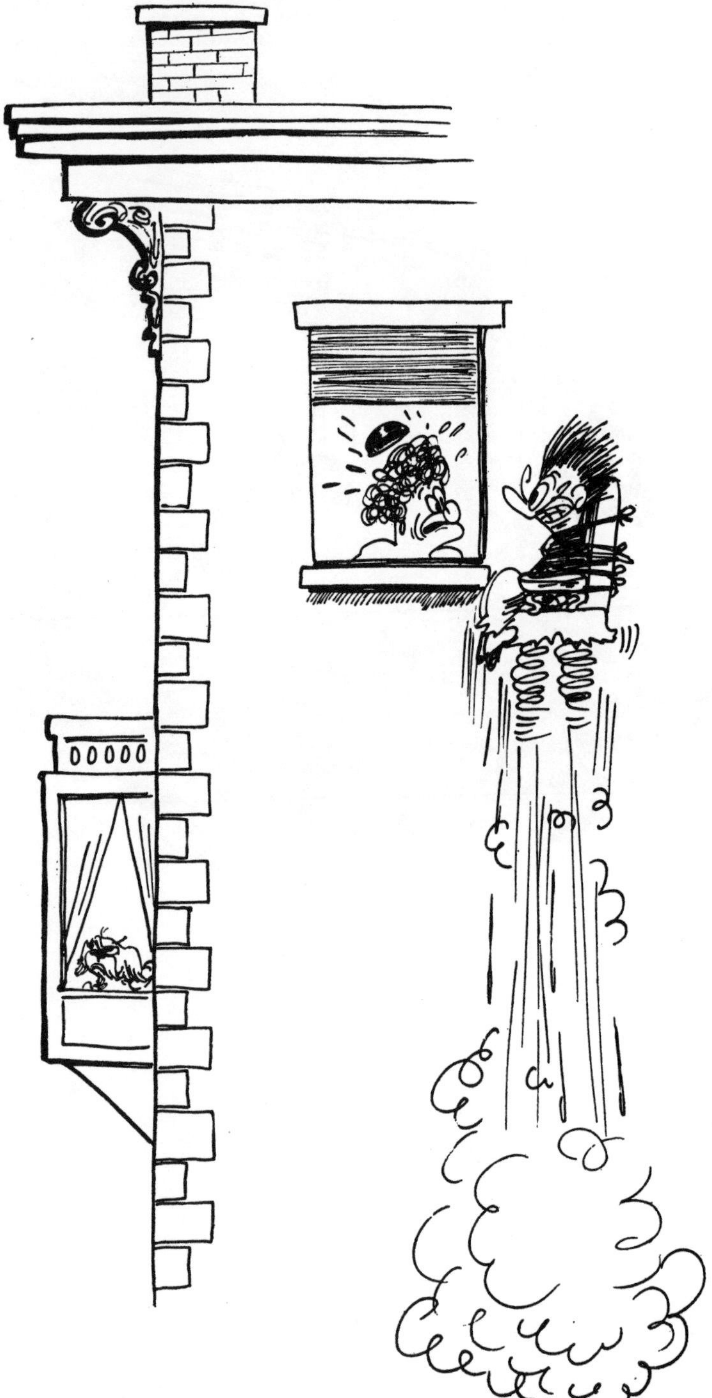

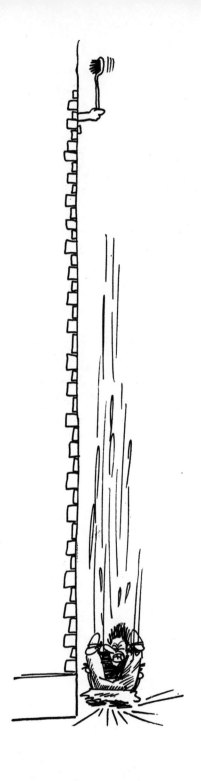

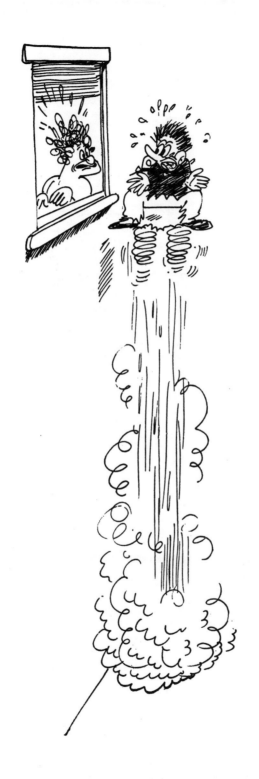

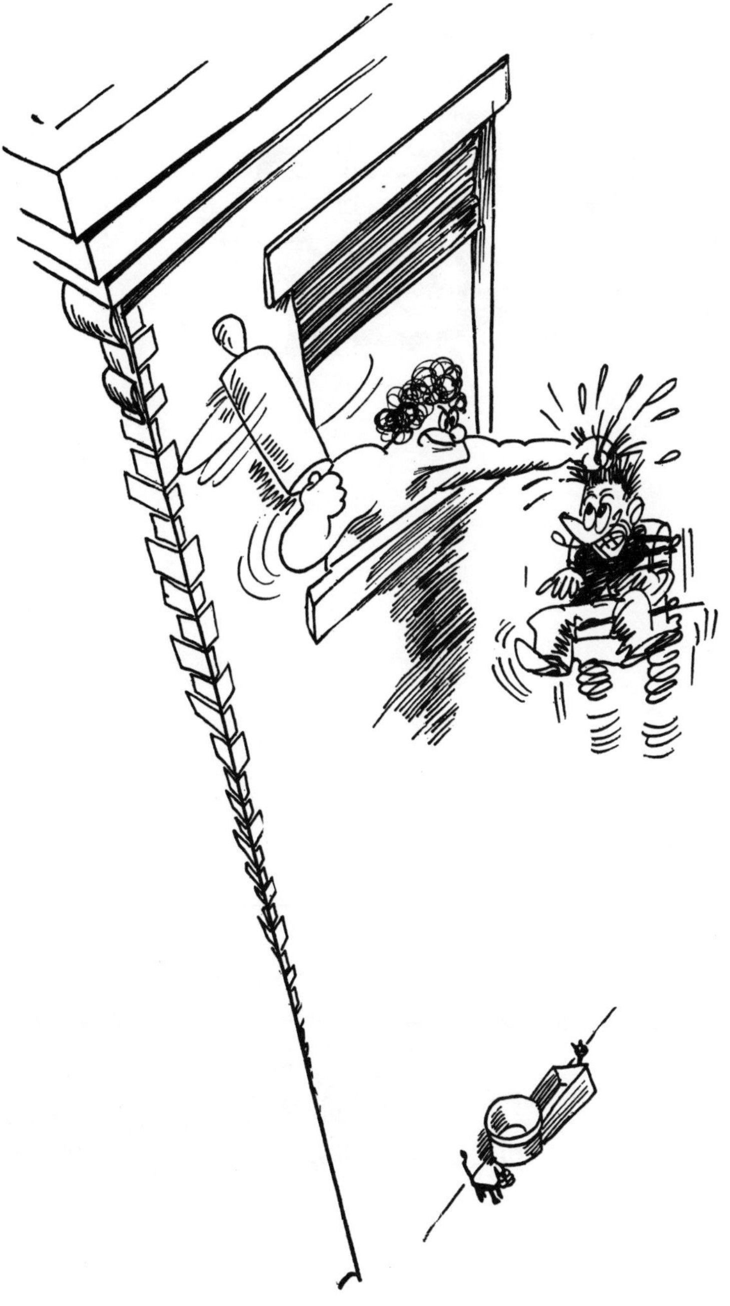

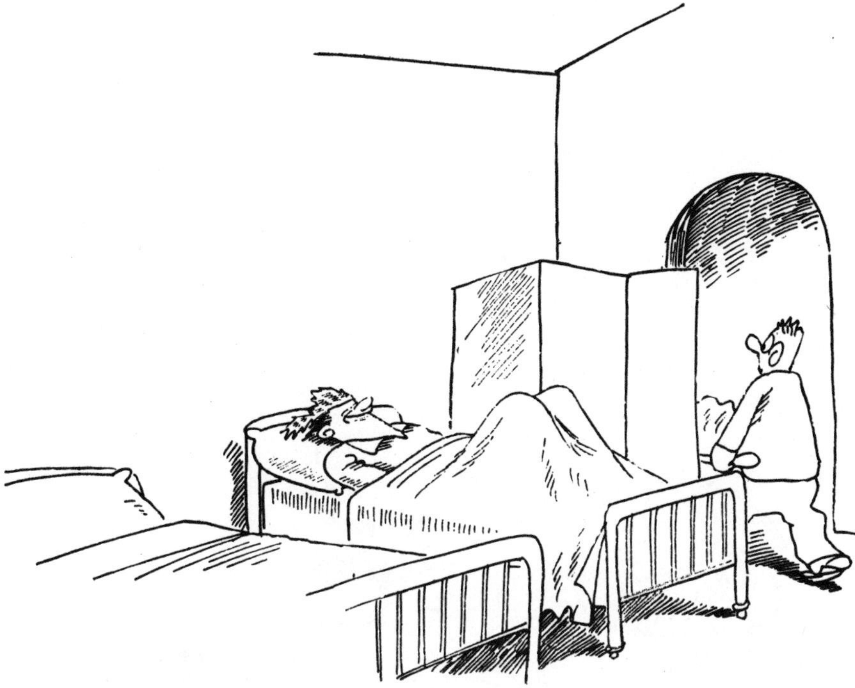

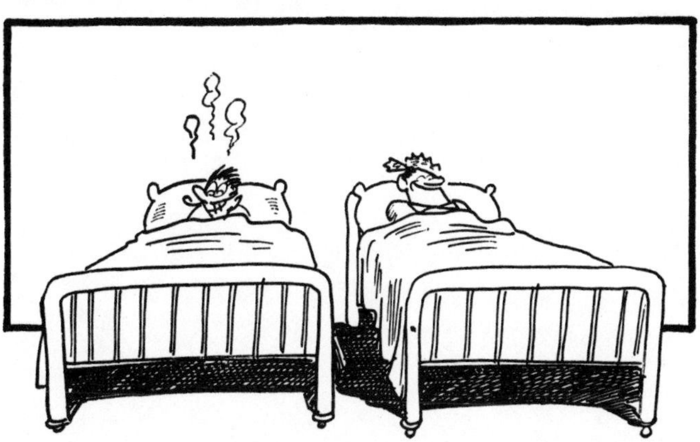

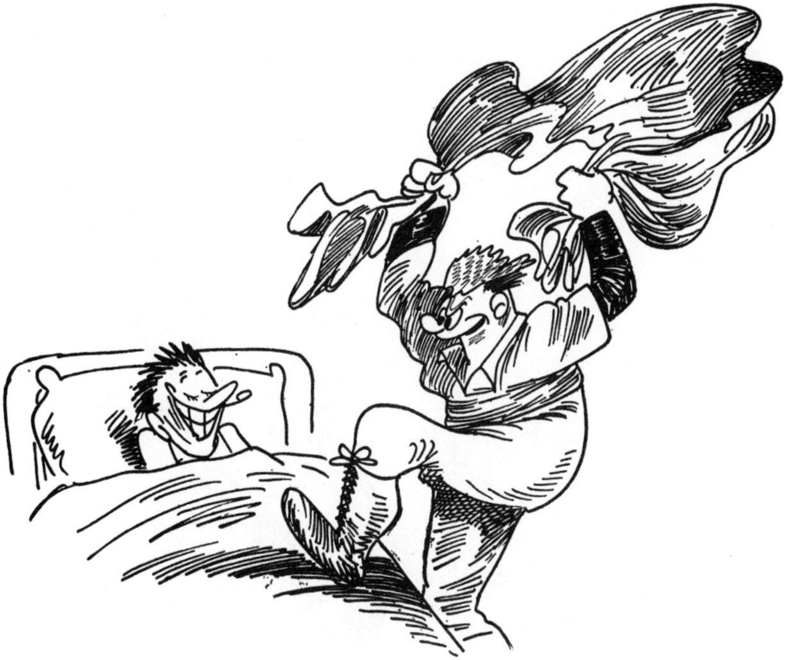

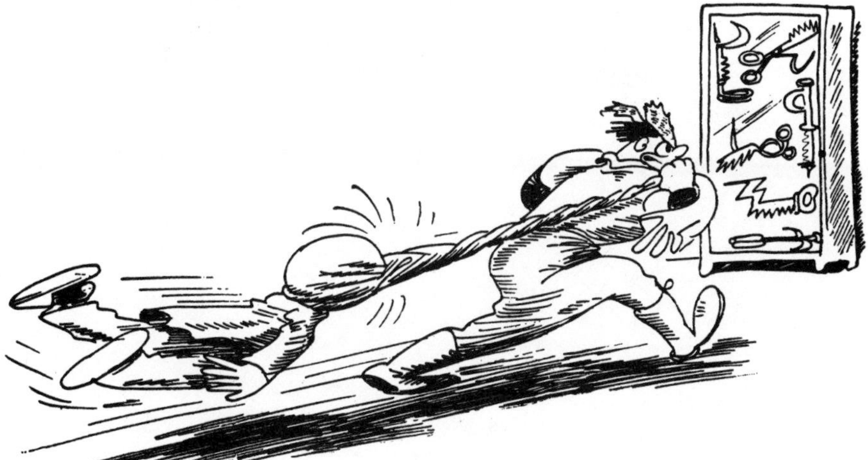

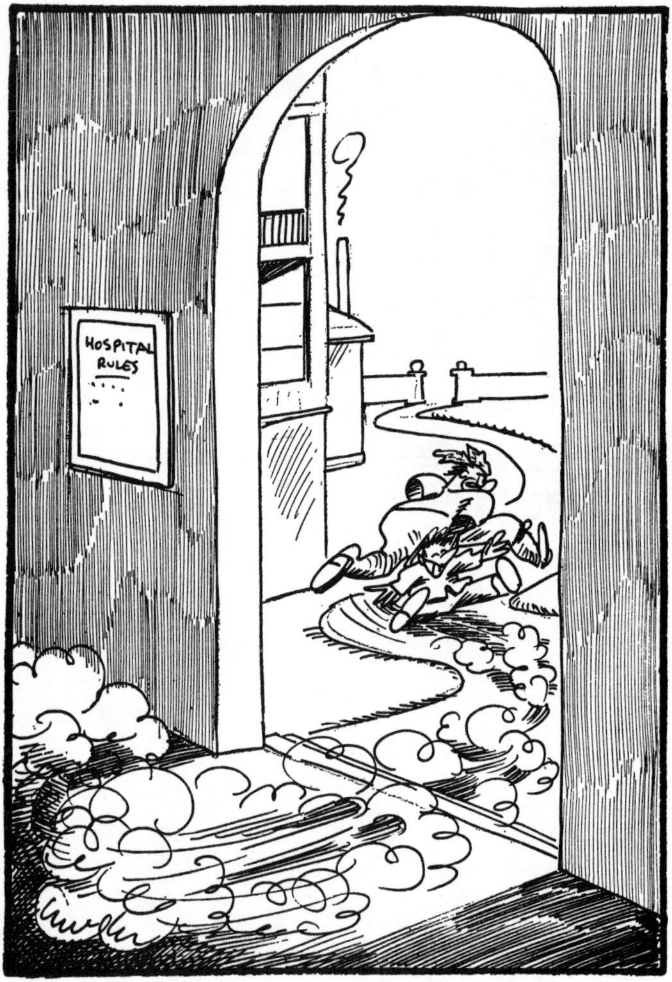
HOSPITAL
RULES

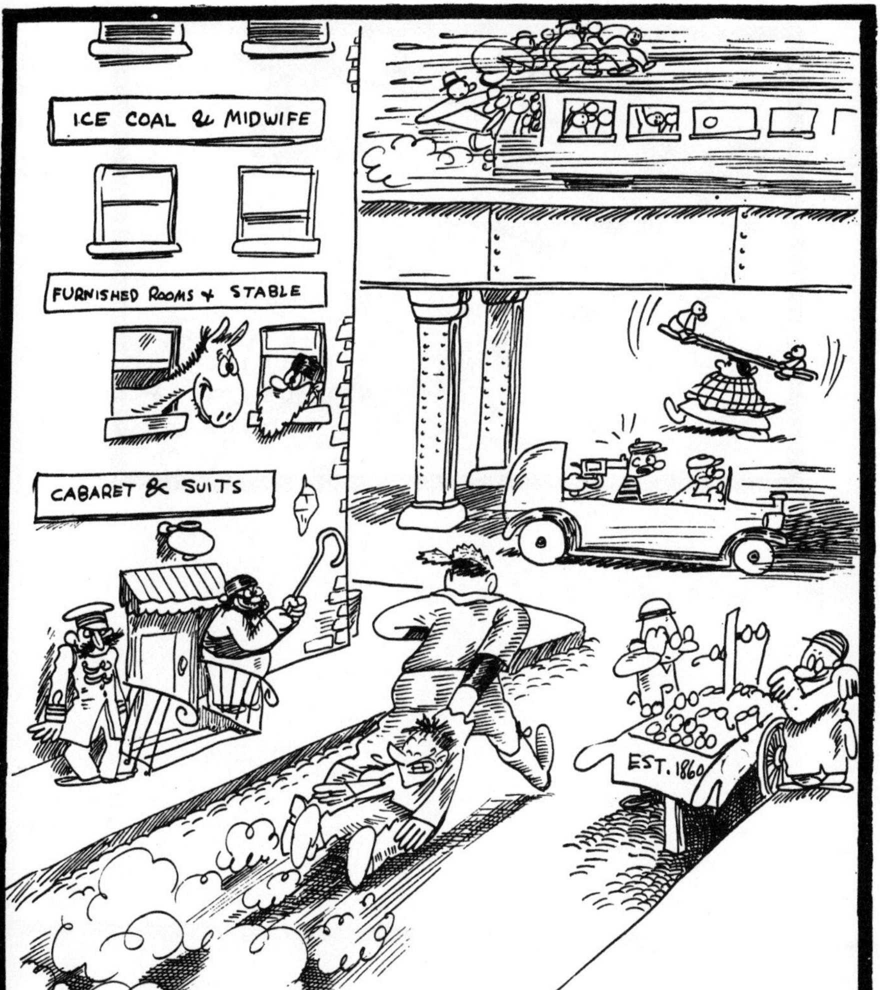
ICE COAL & MIDWIFE
FURNISHED ROOMS & STABLE
CABARET & SUITS
EST. 1860

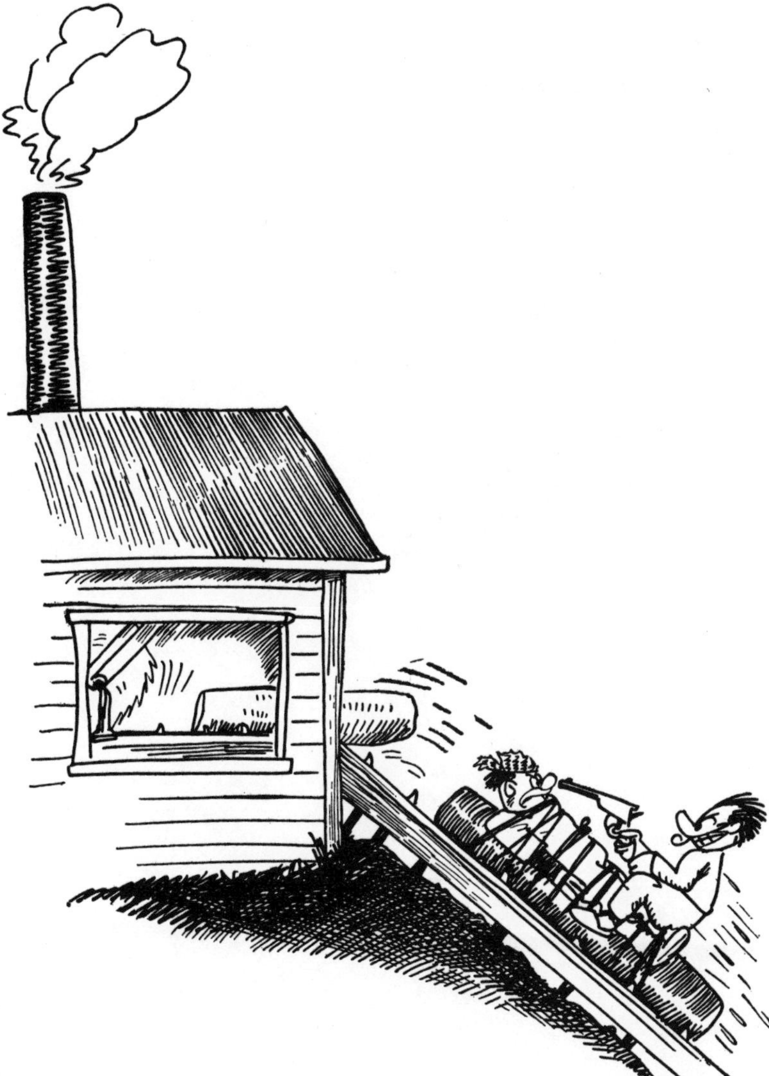

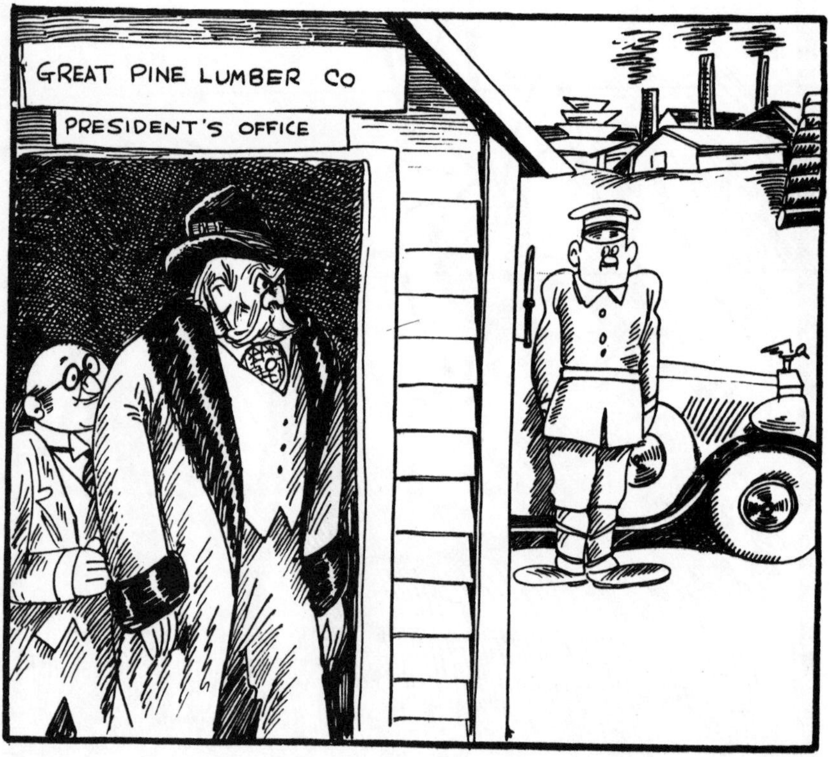
GREAT PINE LUMBER CO
PRESIDENT'S OFFICE

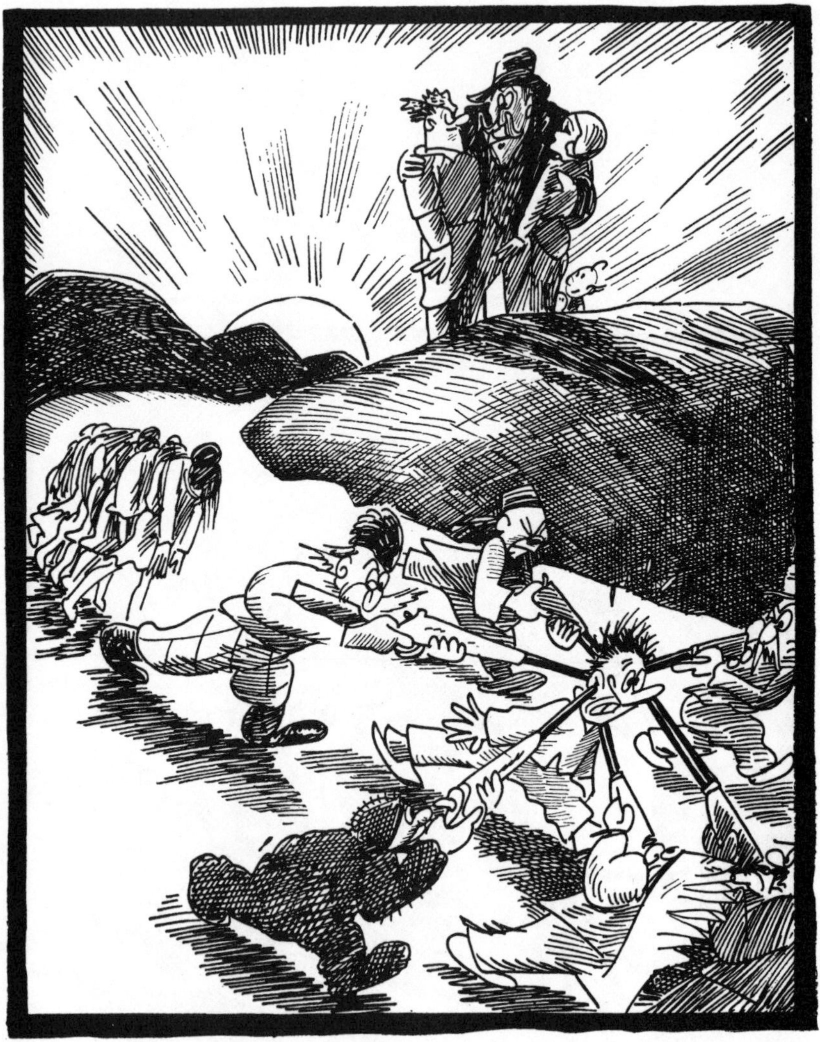

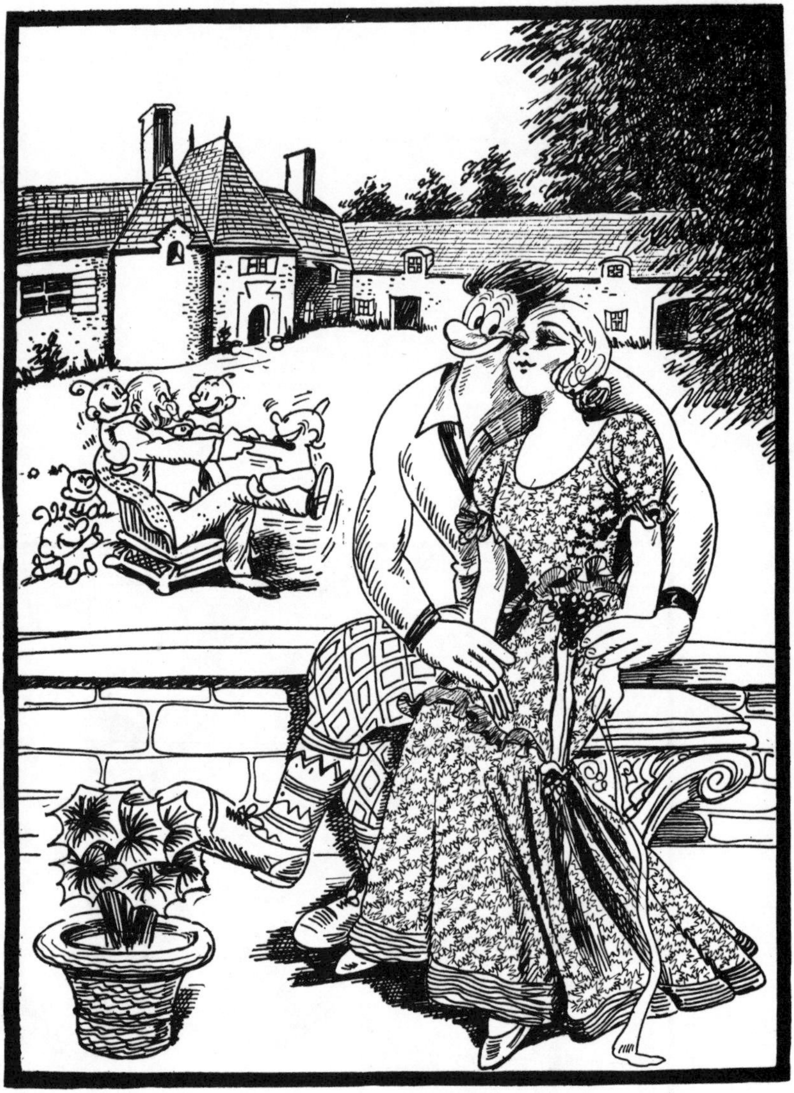

MILT GROSS